The *How-To*
of *being a*
WORKING MOTHER

Belinda Henwood

with Illustrations by Paul Stanish

Angus&Robertson
An imprint of HarperCollins*Publishers*

Angus & Robertson
An imprint of HarperCollins*Publishers*, Australia

First published in Australia in 1995

HarperCollins*Publishers*
25 Ryde Road, Pymble, Sydney NSW 2073, Australia
31 View Road, Auckland 10, New Zealand
77–85 Fulham Palace Road, London W6 8JB, United Kingdom
Hazelton Lanes, 55 Avenue Road, Suite 2900, Toronto, Ontario M5R 3L2
and 1995 Markham Road, Scarborough, Ontario M1B 5M8, Canada
10 East 53rd Street, New York NY 10032, USA

National Library of Australia Cataloguing-in-Publication data:

Henwood, Belinda.
The how-to of being a working mother.
   ISBN 0 207 18817 3.
1.Working mothers - Life skills guides. 2.Work and family.
3. Child rearing. I.Title.
646.700852

Cover illustration by Paul Stanish
Internal illustrations by Paul Stanish

Printed in Hong Kong

9 8 7 6 5 4 3 2 1
95 96 97 98 99

Contents

for help. Don't keep quiet. Take special care of yourself. Your support systems. Avoid the negatives. Double doses of guilt. Remember the positives

Chapter Seven

Chapter Eight

Chapter Nine

Chapter Ten

Chapter Eleven

Chapter Twelve

To Jacob, who has made it all possible

Introduction

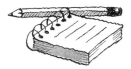

I am the kind of person who has never really planned ahead. I always admired people who decided at an early age what career path they'd take, when they'd marry and how many children they'd have. I've often wondered what it would feel like to be so sure.

The only thing I worked out early on was that I wanted to have a child — or children — but, again, I didn't know if I wanted two until I'd seen what having one was like. For some reason the clearest and most important of my life choices dates from when I was 13 — not that I was either ready or in a position to do anything about it then. Since that age I never questioned that I would be a parent but, at the same time, I can't remember ever questioning that I would work.

I mightn't have had any idea what I would be working at — and I have meandered from job to job and even career to career — but I always assumed that I would work. Partly because I have always thought of myself as being financially self-sufficient and partly because whatever I work at is a passion for me and an integral part of my life.

I am not a mother who is totally relaxed with babies because I'm anxious about their unspoken needs. I am not a mother who can work easily with small children around because I feel their distraction too strongly. And I am not a mother who could stay at home with my son day after day even though he is most important to me.

So I was eager to start my part-time work from home when he was six months old. Being aware of childcare pressures, my partner and I booked into several childcare centres when I was pregnant, but a year later we still hadn't climbed our way to the top of the waiting lists.

A friend I met in the last months of pregnancy (and who lived a few streets away) was returning to part-time work at the same time. She wasn't wanting to send her son to day care so we decided to share a nanny who would look after both children at her home so that I could work away quietly at mine. For 12 months our two boys revelled in each other's company and formed the basis of a loyal and lasting friendship. They had a series of three minders over the year who all brought them quite different things in terms of their interaction, show of affection and stimulation, and I thank them for the wonderful sense of security and trust of adults that they gave our children.

With my part-time salary, it was difficult times for us financially but we were in the bind where I couldn't look for full-time work without full-time care. When we were finally offered a place in an extended hours work-based childcare centre attached to my partner's workplace we grabbed it and I was lucky enough to get a six-month full-time contract job almost immediately.

Fortunately, I didn't have to go through the trauma that I saw in other mothers when their children didn't want to be parted from them. It was made easy for me because my son, Jacob, took to childcare like a duck to water. The centre staff asked me to stay for the first morning while he settled in but we all decided after an hour, when he still hadn't given me a second glance, that my time was up.

I was also extremely lucky that I felt the childcare centre was a wonderful place — brimming with loving staff and the social and intellectual stimulation my son thrived on. He was thrilled to arrive in the mornings and reluctant to leave in the evenings.

So, you can see, that early on what I had to come to terms with was not his distress at our separation but my learning to let go and not be hurt by his independence. For me, it was having to 'brave it' when his favourite carer became 'Mummy' for awhile and I was 'Minny'.

My son is much the same person at the age of 12. He's just gone off on a week-long holiday camp, asking me please not to phone to see if he's all right as my calls interrupt the meals. When I told him that ringing was a way of showing him that I care about him he explained simply that he knows that I care, so there's no need to phone. So now I phone his friend's mother to find out via their calls how he is.

From the childcare centre to an extended hours preschool, to school and before and after care, and to vacation care — we've seen them all. So used to the notion of working parents was he, that for many years it seems he thought that only the children of working parents went to school and that the others got to stay at home!

Since he was three years old I have been a single parent and for many of those years we have dealt with the demands of full-time work and full-time care. Now he's 12 and for the first time I feel that it's important for me to be at home for him. He's outgrown the appeal of after-school care and vacation-care centres and he wants to spend time playing with his dog and just mooching around. I also see this as an important age for me to be there and I am very fortunate in being able to move my work home.

I know that this isn't the usual pattern and that a lot of women choose to be at home during the preschool years. Some women don't want to stay at home at any stage and others do but are forced by circumstances to return to the full-time workforce.

It goes to show that not all our experiences as working mothers are the same. How can they be when we are such different people with different beliefs and responses and correspondingly different children with their own reactions? Nevertheless, there are things we have in common and we can identify to some extent with each other's situations.

It's not the same world we grew up in and there aren't any blueprints for us to follow. We have to work out, as working women in this day and age, how to balance the full plate of running a home, having a family, maintaining a marriage and paying attention to friends. And that's before we find the time to exercise and look after ourselves, let alone the time to read a book like this. What's more, we expect straight A's for everything and to measure up to our own expectations of doing it all well all of the time without bowing under the pressure.

Hopefully you will find some of the suggestions in this book useful or, at least, they'll lead you to think about developing your own strategies. You'll find some solutions for the day-to-day problems that arise — like total exhaustion, choosing childcare, homework hassles and getting your partner to do his share of the housework without turning into a nag. You'll also finds ways of dealing with the emotional issues — like letting go of some of our traditional roles and sharing the responsibilities for home and family as well as coping with the inevitable guilt of being a working mother.

The most important thing I've learnt over the past 13 years is balance. In order to do all the things that I want to do in my life and do them to my own satisfaction, I try to keep a balance. I make sure I pay attention to all the important parts of my life — my son, my family, my friends, my work, myself — on a regular basis. Sometimes one will demand a little more — my son will get sick or have problems at school or all my deadlines will come at once — but I consciously keep the other areas ticking, knowing that it makes for a much smoother ride in the end.

It's impossible for us to get inside each other's heads, let alone each other's hearts which is where our feelings about our children dwell. There is no right or wrong and certainly no rules about how we should live our lives but there are experiences we can share. By writing this book I am hoping to bring to you some of the benefits that both my son and I have had and the lessons we have learnt from me being a working mother.

CHAPTER 1

BALANCING THE WORLD OF A WORKING MOTHER

Have you ever pulled out a piece of paper from a folder in a meeting to discover it's your shopping list? Or dug deep down in your bag for a clean tissue but only scored a Matchbox car? Do you find yourself cooking the cake for tomorrow's fundraising stall at midnight and then falling asleep and dreaming of having a wife? One that stays at home while you go out to work?

Welcome to the world of working mothers

Your work might take various forms — full-time, part-time, casual, self-employed, in an office or from home. Your reasons for working will differ: some of you don't really need the money but want to work; some of you don't really need the money but not working would mean a reduction in your material standard of living; and some of you have to work in order to support yourself and your children.

Whatever your choice, or lack of choice, you'll find that all working mothers face similar dilemmas and have largely the same practical problems, although these vary in degree depending on your financial resources and the kind of support you have or can buy. However, whether you're making ends meet or enjoying a large surplus, your work has benefits for you: it brings you financial rewards; it improves your self-esteem; it gives you the opportunity to meet people; and, usually, it provides some mental stimulation. The other side of it is you may well feel tired, pressured and guilty for most of your waking hours.

While many of you dream of winning the lottery so that you can either stop working or be able to buy the back-up and support that you want, most would almost certainly rather work part-time with full-time benefits (like a full-time salary) so as to be able to more easily balance your home and working lives.

My ideal would be to be a full-time working mother with flexible hours and the authority to control those hours, as well as the financial security to buy the back-up support I need. I would still work because it makes me a happier person which makes me a better mother.'

Some of you are new to the game and want to find out as much as you can about it and others are discovering that different ages and stages bring completely new things to think about. You'll find that you can learn a lot from other working mothers who have all developed their individual approaches to their very individual ways of life.

One thing's for sure, the majority of working mothers aren't the stereotypes that stride across the pages of women's magazines. You are not all overly ambitious or regarded as successful but you can still be invigorated by the challenges that your lives hold and the way your different roles can contribute to one another.

The different roles we play

If you think about roles in plays or films, they involve different scenes, different characters and different scripts, which all involve different ways of communicating and different expectations. During the course of the day you may well be required to move smoothly between your many roles and be a mother, a wife, a lover, a friend, a worker, a daughter, an active member of the local or school community, and maybe an ex-wife as well.

Sometimes your roles overlap and sometimes they are quite separate. It's no mean feat to meet all the demands of any one role, let alone find the time and energy to meet many.

The changing world we live in

It's likely that you are at an age when your children are young and dependent at the same time that your aging parents require your attention and, for many, there is a conflict between nurturing your family and having to earn a living. While this conflict isn't new, it is one that is fairly unfamiliar. It's quite a different world from the one you grew up in — with most of your mothers having more clearly defined roles and different expectations — and this means that you don't have the benefit of previous experience to fall back on and to draw from. So not only do you have to deal with the dilemma of being a working mother, but you have to work out how to do it as you go along.

It's a world, too, where people are less certain because things and opinions change so fast. Just looking at the number of books about parenting and childcare would make any modern-day parent feel confused if not inadequate. And that's before you even begin to try to follow and understand the constantly changing theories.

You are going to work but, at the same time, you still tend to organise the home and to take responsibility for the family. Because of the notion of the nuclear family, you also now tend to do it pretty much alone because there aren't the extended families of the past and the support and information they brought with them. Nor are there the same community networks.

Some have partners to help but many of you now find yourselves on your own, running a household and bringing up a family single-handed.

Some of you are dealing with blending two families and all that entails. Some of you have found that your partners have taken on more of the household and child-rearing duties as you have moved into the workforce but many men, like many working women, are still feeling their way and seeking solutions.

> 'I don't have much choice with my financial situation but, apart from that, I also enjoy being able to give my children as good a start in life as possible. That takes money.'

Life with no margins

Most of you lead such busy lives that there are no margins — no room for problems and no space for mistakes or complications. Each member of the family lives to a tight schedule during the working week and, often, on weekends even leisure time is highly organised. What would once have been seen as the highs and lows of everyday life now take on much more significance because there is no extra space to deal with them.

In this hectic life you also expect to find the time for finetuning. You want to be an attentive and loving parent, spouse, sibling, daughter and friend. You want to enjoy a social life, be healthy and exercise. You want to relax. And you want to do it all well. And that's before you go to work and attend to the domestic scene — including paying the bills, making dental appointments and giving the cat his worm tablets.

'My reaction whenever the children get ill is to panic. I feel like I am living on a knife edge. When my daughter was sick and home from school recently I felt totally torn and a nervous wreck.'

Most women don't even have the fantasy of wanting to do everything because the reality of trying to be a superwoman comes at too high a price. But even if you accept that you aren't an overachiever, you find that, when there is so much for you to do, you fall into the trap of spreading yourself too thin.

Advice that tells you that you need to recognise the limits of your energy and resources and acknowledge when you are taking on too much rarely makes much impact. To simplify and slow down is easier said than done. Where would you start and how would you go about it? After all, you can't very well stop making school lunches, paying the bills or doing the washing.

Focus on what matters

When you take it from the other direction and focus on what matters most to you, rather than on what your limits are, then you'll find that the unnecessary more easily falls away and you can learn to say 'no' to things that aren't absolutely essential to you and your family's well-being. By paying more attention to and ruthlessly devoting your time and energy to what's most precious, you can simplify your life.

If you feel that you suffer from fatigue and lack of time, try sitting down and making a list of what is important to you. Your list might include things like:

- feeling confident that you are paying enough attention to your children's needs — both inside and outside the home;

- making your home a haven that you want to spend time in with your family;

- maintaining the quality of your relationship with your partner;

- having a smoothly running household — getting the essential jobs done with a minimum amount of drama;

- feeling satisfied that you have put in a good day's work;

- feeling that you have things reasonably well planned and under control — avoiding doing things at the last minute and in a panic;

- being able to spend time with your friends and family;

- feeling good about yourself and how well you treat yourself by paying attention to your health, stress levels and exercise.

Then look at your calendar and what you have planned for the next few weeks. For practice, see how they fit your list. Then when new things come up, you can be prepared to say 'no' — without guilt — to what doesn't contribute to your list. While you might feel as though you are being too harsh, until you actively start to change how you are living you are going to continue to feel flat out and fatigued. It might mean saying 'no' to a social engagement with a group of work acquaintances in order to have an evening out with dear friends or a quiet evening at home with the family. Remind yourself that you are doing it for your own benefit and for your family.

> Being a working mother is very fulfilling but it comes at a high price. You always feel you aren't doing anything as well as you should and you are constantly tired. The highs are the pleasures both work and motherhood bring; the lows are the lack of personal time and the constant frenetic pace.'

Ask for help

Often as a working mother you feel that you should be able to cope single-handedly, but you need to remind yourself that it's your situation and lifestyle that make it difficult and it's not a question of your not being able to cut the mustard.

Don't be afraid to seek support and ask for help. Don't look at it as admitting defeat but as installing a safety net. You'll find that it's invaluable to have friends or family to call on when you are sick, need a hand or just want someone to talk to. It will save you a lot of emotional energy knowing that you have a backstop and it will also help your children to develop a sense of community.

You also need to get your partner and children involved in the running of the home. From a very early age, children can begin to contribute by tidying their toys and rooms and doing simple cleaning jobs. Perhaps your partner is still in training and you need some tips on giving him encouragement awards. Ideally, what you are working towards here is for other family members to do their full share (which will also change with a child's age) rather than for them to think that they are helping you. Remember that you doing it all isn't doing anyone any favours, including you.

Asking for help and getting others involved also means that you will have to learn to let go of the control a little. When you take on a new role, it's time to think seriously about letting one go. You may find that it is just as difficult for you to relinquish a responsibility as it is to get others to take it up, but in order to have the time and energy to enjoy all the facets of your life as fully as possible, you'll have to give up on some aspects a little. It may well be time to share the domestic domain more.

Balance your roles

Living the life of a working mother is often referred to as juggling because of the many roles involved, but if that's not what you consider your best circus act, it's probably not a description that will fill you with confidence. Juggling means that everything's in the air and it implies too little control over what you are doing — after all, if you drop one ball or skittle then the others will fall.

A less scary image is to think about balance. If you have balance in all the areas of your life, when one tips a little (as it inevitably will), the others don't necessarily have to slide too. Also, it makes you conscious of how you approach these areas, paying attention to all the aspects of your life that are important to you — your family, your work, your relatives, your friends and yourself. It makes for a calmer, more considered approach that will leave you feeling more in control.

If you work at maintaining this balance, then nothing is going to suffer from serious neglect. You aren't going to be overwhelmed by any one aspect or feel that it is really getting out of hand. You'll find that if one area seems to be sliding, you automatically look to the others to make sure they are all okay. Even though sometimes you might feel as though you are only holding on by a thin thread, the important thing is that you don't feel that you are losing your grip altogether.

Look at your various roles and consciously divide your time up every day so that you pay some attention to each of them. Try to maintain a balance between them and you'll find you can keep everything on a pretty even keel. Some days, some things will require more attention than others — whether it's your child having problems at school, your aging mother or your work — but that's the nature of everyday life and it doesn't have to send you into a spin. Other days, some parts will look like an absolute disaster because the childminder's sick, your partner's out of town and you have an important presentation to give, but then, on those days you can reassure yourself with the parts of your life that are going well. (If you can't think of any it's time to go to bed and have a good sleep.)

Pay attention to each role

Think about how you allot your time each working day and consider whether you are paying attention directly to what really matters and to the things that will make your family life and home life run smoothly. Your list may be a very simple one.

- Spend the hours when you get home from work with your children.

- Spend time with your partner when the children have gone to bed.

- Make a couple of phone calls to family and friends.

- Attend to some family 'administration', like paying bills, making appointments
and so on.

- Do some form of exercise, even if it's taking a walk around the block.

- Do some domestic chores, like ironing tomorrow's clothes or cleaning the bath.

- Find some time for yourself — to relax in your clean bath or do some yoga.

A way to remind yourself of how balanced your life is to ask yourself every morning what you would do today if you only had three months to live. The funny thing is that you'll find that you are only slightly tempted to hop on the next plane to Paris. Strangely enough, you're likely to pay more attention to the little things of life, like making dentist's appointments and taking the dog to the vet.

Remind yourself of the positives

'How lucky I am because I can look forward to going to work in the morning and coming home to my children at night.'

'He is thrilled to see me when I pick him up and I am thrilled to see him.'

There is no formula and no quick-fix solution for being a working mother. Our lives are too complex and varied for that so it's a matter of finding what's right for you. While there's no straightforward set of answers, at the same time remember that there isn't a strict set of rules you have to live by.

Creating balance in your life in order to enjoy the elements of family and work is not going to happen overnight and it's not going to happen effortlessly. It will involve time and energy, which are just what you feel you don't have. In order, though, to feel consistently good about how you are living your life and to feel as though you aren't missing out on what matters, you'll have to make some changes. You'll need to make the time to be with your family, with your friends, to relax and to exercise.

'The good thing for me about returning to work was that it made me get organised, get into a routine, get fit and keep on top of my health. It can sure give you a lot of bounce.'

As a working mother you need to safeguard your physical and mental health by striving for a balanced life. Some days it will seem easier than others so you'll need to stick with the positive thinking on the bad days and remind yourself that:

- time away from a small child can be a benefit to you both;
- variation and space are not only beneficial but vital to some people, especially when it comes to mothering because it is such a constant job;
- your child can benefit from the variety of experience and people and will develop a sense of independence;
- a working mother can provide a useful role model for your child, preparing him for the changing family structures that he will encounter in his lifetime;
- there are financial benefits for you;
- it is good for your self-esteem;
- you can enjoy the different rhythms of home and work and take pleasure in the difference in priorities.

'Sometimes when I have a really rotten day at work I come home to my family and leave all the bad stuff behind. Apart from the fact that I don't have the time to dwell on the problems, this helps put things in perspective and I recognise what's important in my life.'

CHAPTER 2

Take the time, make the time

You spend your days ruled by your watch — getting to work on time, getting to childcare on time and doing a thousand things in between. You fall into bed every night exhausted, your eyes closed before your head touches the pillow. You've crossed five things off your 'to do' list, only to find that they've been replaced by six more.

Where did the time go?

If you feel that you have less time now that you're a working mother, it's because it's true. If you were to make a list of the major things you have taken on in your life in the last five years — like having a baby, renovating a house, getting a new job — and then were to make a list of the things you have resigned from or given up, you'd probably find your commitments have multiplied.

The additions always look attractive at the time (and, indeed, they usually are welcome) but in that first phase of euphoria you rarely think through what is entailed and what changes you need to make in order to find time for them. The way you managed your time before you were a working mother may be quite different from what you need to do now.

In so many aspects of this way of life, there's no one there to tell you how to handle them or help you find the answers. It's a discovery and learning process, so don't get impatient with yourself if you don't seem to have it all together right from the start or if you change your mind about what works. What's important is finding systems that suit you. Everyone has quite different ways of managing their time depending on their personalities, and there's no right or wrong. These are just some alternatives to choose from.

- Be first up in the morning and use the time when no one else is around to get a few extra things done.

- Sleep a bit longer in the morning and use the quiet time at night when everyone else has gone to bed.

- Write a 'to do' list the night before of all you need to do the next day and check each task off as you complete it.

- Take each day as it comes and wing it.

Working out what suits

There are some questions you can ask yourself that will help you work out how to make the best use of your time. You may find that you haven't thought about some of these things before or, perhaps, you may find that it's time to change your habits if what you're doing isn't working. Here are a few things to think about.

- What's your peak energy time? Early mornings, afternoons, or evenings? Are you using it to your advantage?

- Are you best following a routine or do you like variety in your schedule?

- Do you find a daily 'to do' list effective or do you work better to a more long-range plan like a weekly list?

- Would you prefer to tackle big tasks in big blocks of time or is it better for you to break them up into smaller bits? Would you rather clean out a whole cupboard or take it a shelf at a time? For that matter, do you ever clean out the cupboard? If not, is it because when you think about the whole cupboard, it stops you from cleaning it out altogether? Would it be better to think about a shelf at a time, which is far less daunting? And how about that report you have to write?

- Do you consciously make breaks in your day so that you can change gear and activities? Move smoothly from the pace of work to home?

- How do you spend your lunchtime — do you leave your desk? Do you take a break from work and use it to exercise (even if it's a walk outside) or to run errands?

- Do you prefer to fit your errands and chores into the working week so that the weekends can be free for family and friends?

Managing your time

In working out what suits you, sometimes it's just a matter of changing some simple things in your life.

• Use your highest energy time to its best advantage.

• Schedule less taxing tasks — like returning phone calls or filing — for your low energy time.

• Plot a quiet time in the day for things that need planning and peace.

• When you have a lot on your plate, divide the tasks up and allot them amounts of time so that you are less likely to feel a sense of panic about any particular one.

• Keep a list of things 'to do', which allows you to keep less in your head, and use your list to help you set priorities.

• Remember that you don't always have to be busy. Ignore the pressure to make every minute count. Is it wasting time to notice that the spring flowers are blooming or that the autumn leaves have fallen?

Ways to lighten the load

A working mother's endless 'to do' lists mean being constantly under pressure to do more than one thing at a time — testing the spelling while driving your child to school, writing your shopping list while you're waiting for the bus, or even writing in a journal at the end of the day listing all the things you've forgotten to do or the self-improvements that you need to make. At the same time, you keep hearing advice to slow down, prioritise, and devote more time to your family and to yourself.

Let go of what's not important to you they say, but it's not always easy. It's not as though you can suddenly decide that vacuuming doesn't matter any more, tempting as it might be.

What is easy is to forget what matters most to you. Occasionally, it's important to take the time to question what you are doing and where you are going. With so many things to think about it's easy to lose track of some of them and to lose sight of where you're going. A daily 'to do' list can take the pressure off remembering and it can help you decide what matters most. Before you begin a task, ask yourself how essential it is and how urgent. Or whether there's someone else in the family you can get to do it.

How important are those tasks that still haven't been done after a few days? If you're feeling pushed by all the things you have to do, then you have to be the one to take the step to get off the treadmill. If you're overbooked and overtired, you're the one that's responsible because you're the only one who can determine what a reasonable load for you is. There will always be plenty to do but it's up to you to learn how to say 'no'.

Try being ruthless. Look hard at what you have to do. What can you delegate to someone else? Who can you ask for help? What can you cross off your list and not do at all? What would you say 'no' to next time?

A home running like clockwork?

The last thing you want after the time pressures of the working day is to come home to a clock-ruled regime. On the other hand, if you organise your home life a bit you'll find that things can run smoothly without being overly rigid. See if some of these suggestions suit you.

- Have a noticeboard hanging in the kitchen or family room — wherever is most practical — where school notices, emergency phone numbers and any reminders can be pinned.

- Have a household calendar to record the family's commitments and appointments. You may also need to transfer these to your own diary and vice versa. If you're an organisational freak you can have different coloured pens for each member of the family for the calendar so a glance can tell you who's doing what.

- Schedule into your day the blocks of time that you need for regular activities such as exercise, preparing for the following day, time with the children, homework and housework.

- Try to make sure that belongings have their own storage place and are put away so that they are always easy to find. It's a good habit for you to learn if you aren't a particularly tidy person, it's great training for the kids, and it will save a lot of frayed tempers.

- Give every member of the family a tote bag or an in-tray for their own pieces of important paper. Make older children responsible for going through their own and keeping them in order and under control.

- Start up folders for bills, correspondence, receipts and the like and go through each one on a weekly basis, attending to the items as necessary. Once dealt with, file things away in a concertina file. It can be infuriating to have to spend time looking for a receipt when something has to be returned to a shop or for repairs and so much simpler if you know where to put your hands on it.

- Don't feel bad about using a telephone answering machine when you're at home. It can be very handy, for example, when you're bathing a baby and don't want to leave her alone. It also can give you an opportunity to spend uninterrupted time with your children or by yourself. Remember, you can always call back.

Avoiding the morning mayhem

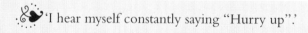 'I hear myself constantly saying "Hurry up".'

When you have a house full of busy people, each with their own time pressures to meet, morning can mean madness. To help give you all a good start to your day try these tips.

- Every evening prepare as much as you can for the following day.
- If you like, pack the lunches with non-perishables the night before and you can even prepare and freeze the sandwiches.

- Make sure clothes are ironed and ready to wear, with accessories organised too.

- When they are old enough, get your children to put their clothes or uniforms out ready to wear — preferably putting things like shoes, belts and ties in a regular place so they are easy to find.

- Put any of tomorrow's essentials — like your gym bag or your daughter's tennis racquet — near the front door ready to go.

- Check that your children have completed all their homework and packed their school bags.

- Make sure any permission slips or other correspondence has been signed and is in the packed school bag.

- Try getting all the family up a little earlier so that there is a slower, more relaxed start to the day.

- Give the kids their own alarm clocks so that you aren't responsible for waking them up and getting them out of bed.

- If there is a bathroom pile-up, make a schedule and give everyone a time limit. Put a timer in the bathroom to help keep them on their toes.

- Checklists for the kids of what they have to do can save you having to remind them.

- Have a regular routine of breakfast and getting ready without distractions. This may well be the time to say 'no' to television.

- Make breakfasts simple and as do-it-yourself as possible.

Of course, your best made plans aren't necessarily going to get your child moving — but neither is your telling her to hurry up all the time. As difficult as it may be, sometimes you have to let her learn to understand the consequences instead of turning yourself into a nag.

Leave her alone one morning and just get yourself ready so you can leave the house on time. (You might want to warn them at work that you have a trick up your sleeve and you could be late the next morning.) Then you can either take her half-dressed to school or leave the house without her and hide around the corner for five minutes — because that's all it'll take for her to panic — or wait calmly outside until she is ready and let her bear the consequences at school for being late.

On the other hand, if you have a week of smooth sailing, why not occasionally reward yourselves with a video and a takeaway pizza at the end of the working week, letting all the family know that there can sometimes be extra benefits from cooperating?

Quality time — just another worry?
The whole notion of quality time can set any mother off on a worry spree. What does it mean and how well do you provide it? Is your quality time as good as your next-door neighbour's? Does it mean you can't ever be in a bad mood or get cross with your child when you're occupying the quality time space?

'What's quality time? It always sounds to me as though it's some strange obligation to be enjoying yourself whenever you're alone with your partner and child. Good times can be had quickly and without warning. The thing is to recognise them when they are happening.'

As a working mother, you may feel bad about the fact that you aren't at home but it isn't necessarily the case that children of working mothers spend less time with their parents than children of mothers who stay at home. To offset lost afternoon hours, working parents often spend more time with their children on the weekends and while they do their homework, too.

'At weekends I deliberately find things that we can all do together that are relaxing or good exercise for us. We often go swimming or mountain-bike riding. I never dreamt that I might be spending my weekends fishing but it's a great way for us to unwind and be together on weekends.'

Look at quality time as just another way of saying that you don't have to feel bad about the amount of time you spend (or don't spend) with your child. It's about how you spend the time — the attention you pay her and the fact that you know and she knows that you have set aside time especially for her. Of course, families being families it won't always work out that way and you'll wish you never had some of your so-called quality times together, but you can always make up for it another day.

There'll be days when you come home tired and stressed and when your child comes home tired and stressed and you'll lose your cool. That's life. Don't pressure yourself into thinking you have to be perfect as well as present. Growing up today is about learning to deal with the ups and downs and the stresses and strains of the working world.

Instead of turning quality time into a duty and yet another pressure, think about the spirit of quality time. It's the time when you are together, time that you want to enjoy, time to have fun with your family because you want to be there and not because you feel you have to. See it as time for you to get to know this special person in your life and for her to get to know you — warts and all.

'I don't like to think about "quality time" because when I think it should be happening is most often when I'm at my worst. I would rather just do the best I can to be involved with her as much as possible when we are together, whether she's just sitting on my lap or we are having long reads or conversations with each other.'

Making time together

You'll find that how you spend your time together with your child will vary over the years. Small children are often happy sitting with you and reading a book, playing games or going on an outing to the park. As your child gets older you may want to just talk — discuss the day, her schoolwork or the playground politics, or simply sit and watch television together. It might be learning about the latest additions to the basketball card collection or sitting and playing with Barbie. Because it's about sharing your time, you don't even have to do anything or talk to each other if that's what suits you both.

Most often, working parents find the evenings are the time they set aside for being together with their children. Some partners prefer to share the routine and chores when children are small — one cooks while the other bathes the child, one cleans up while the other reads. Then they take it turn and turn about on different nights. When your child gets older the evening meal together can be a good opportunity to spend some time communicating and sharing the events of the day.

Others find the early mornings spent quietly together can give a good start to the day. It may mean that you have to go to bed earlier but you'll find that you'll all benefit from a more relaxed pace, especially if you have prepared clothes and bags the night before.

Don't feel that you always need to set aside special time — you can also involve your child in your household routines, like watering the garden, doing the washing and the supermarket shopping. Sometimes a working mother's day is more easily divided up into time capsules — now it's time to do the shopping, now it's time to cook dinner, now I'll spend time with the children — but there's no reason why it can't be more integrated. There's no harm in them participating in these activities — although you'll probably find it'll take you longer. But does that really matter when it's all a part of their learning process and also an opportunity for you to spend more time together?

When you're busy you'll need to be careful not to get into the habit of saying to your children 'Not now, later' and later never comes. It can be particularly hard if you are always pressed for time to remember to find the time later. While children have to learn that they can't always have your attention exactly when they want it, they also need to know that you will find time for them and that you will keep your word.

'I am very conscious that when I pick her up from childcare each day that I will then pay attention to her needs for the next couple of hours. I no longer make phone calls to friends or colleagues at that time, and if they call I say I'll ring them later. It's not hard to do when I've been away from her all day, and I look at it as a good way to change from my working pace.'

'We get home at six in the evening and I immediately start to cook my son's dinner because he's tired and hungry. I don't mind if he watches television for that half-hour because it helps him unwind and distracts him while I do the practical stuff. Then he eats, I bath him, and after I've made sure that his homework is done for the following day, we'll read together till he goes to bed at 8.30. Then it's my time.'

The generation gap

Adolescence, if you remember, is that mysterious time when talkative children become silent strangers and parents are the people who drive the car (and drop them at the corner) and sign the cheques. Communication is a closed bedroom door with you but endless telephone conversations with friends. Their personalities slip smoothly back and forth between the ages of 6 and 16.

Despite your being from another planet and, more truthfully, from another generation, you need to maintain some kind of connection. It's up to you to keep the communication channels open — even when it is through closed doors — recognising that this is a natural process of pulling away. You'll need to be there for them — even though they won't be at home — and be available to talk to — even though they won't want to talk to you. If they'll still go out with you, try scheduling some private time away from home, like going to films together, having breakfast or going for a swim.

CHAPTER 3

TIRED AND STRESSED?

You can't remember what it was like to have sex when you were still awake. You prise your eyes open in the morning feeling as though you've only just fallen off after yet another sleepless night. You dread the thought of getting up and everything you have to do. You've found that it's best not to think too much, so you go to make breakfast and discover that you put the iron carefully away in the fridge the night before. To top it off, you drive the kids to school and it's the holidays.

Sleep and how to get it

While it might sound obvious, enough sleep is vital to your energy levels. Most people need between seven and ten hours a night and this is likely to increase when you are pregnant, stressed or depressed.

Of course, there will be times when sleeplessness is inevitable, such as when you have a small baby or your child is sick, but you should find time to make up for it. Perhaps you need to take naps on the weekend, half an hour's rest when you get home, or have an early night while your partner puts the finishing touches to the family's day.

Eating a big meal at night can affect your sleep and going to bed early isn't a good idea for everyone. While some find it a good way to wind down, for others it means a long night in bed but not necessarily a long sleep. Remember, sex is a pretty pleasant way to pass the time.

An occasional night of bad sleep isn't generally a problem, so don't make it worse by worrying about the fact that you aren't sleeping. Remind yourself that you will sleep more soundly the next night to compensate.

'I am resigned to (but not resentful of) the fact that the next few years are for them and I am going to be permanently fatigued.'

SOME SIMPLE INSOMNIA SOLUTIONS

Prolonged insomnia can pose problems and affect your health and wellbeing. You may have difficulty just getting to sleep, wake in the night because of worry or stress, or sleep with someone who snores like a chainsaw and moves around the bed like a bulldozer. Then it's time to look for answers.

When you do wake, instead of worrying about how tired you will feel the next day, get up and make some hot milk, read for awhile, or work on the project that's worrying you.

You might try moving to a quieter, more solitary place to sleep.

Knock-out tips

When getting a good night's sleep really becomes a problem, run yourself a warm (not too hot) bath. When the bath is full, put four drops of any of the following essential oils onto the top of the water:

- valerian
- marjoram
- clary sage
- lemon
- sandalwood

Soak for awhile and then go to bed with a cup of chamomile tea. If you have a burner for essential oils, put it beside the bed, using any of the above oils in it, and read a relaxing book (not a compelling thriller!). If need be, take one or two valerian capsules which you can buy from a health food store. Apart from anything else, the ritual is bound to slow you down and help psych you into sleep.

Your child's sleeping patterns

Apart from stress, the major factor that stops a working mother from sleeping is her adorable child. Sometimes it's inevitable that you have to get up in the night to tend him because of his need for comfort or reassurance, especially when he has bad dreams or is sick. You can't afford, though, to let him develop a habit of disturbing you at night or you'll both be history. It's important for his wellbeing and yours that you encourage him to develop healthy sleeping patterns.

Don't feel responsible if he doesn't go to sleep. It's your responsibility to provide the right environment and to put him to bed in a way that is conducive to sleep, but that's where your responsibility ends. If he can't sleep, it's not your problem and you must not be tempted into spending your evenings coaxing a child to go to sleep. It's unlikely he will want to sleep if he can have the attention of an audience.

The vital element in training your child to sleep undisturbed (or without disturbing you) is consistency. Here are some ground rules.

- Establish a bedtime ritual when he is very small of putting toys away, having a bath, reading a story and perhaps letting him listen to a soothing tape in bed.

- Make sure that his bedroom is conducive to sleep — that it's reasonably quiet and the night-light isn't too bright.

- If he doesn't go to sleep straight away or he wakes in the night, make sure that he understands that he stays in his bed or is returned there promptly.

Symptoms of stress

A certain amount of stress can be positive and help make you function well — because it stimulates and motivates — but when the needle on the gauge goes too far you feel like you'll blow your top. Every little thing that goes wrong becomes a major catastrophe and simple mistakes your children make, like spilling a drink, can set you off screaming.

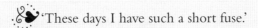 'These days I have such a short fuse.'

There are both physical and emotional signs of stress that you can learn to identify. Listen to your body and learn when it's time to ease up. If you're suffering from an uncomfortable amount of irritability, forgetfulness, crying, anxiety, fatigue, headaches, shoulder and neck tension or insomnia, it's time to de-stress.

Where to start

'I don't have the time to deal with my stress. Getting involved in stress reduction seems like a luxury I can't afford.'

Just a look at your daily 'to do' list is enough to start raising the stress level of even the most relaxed of working mothers, but there are other things that contribute to feelings of burnout. Trying to do too much or more than you need to do can be what pushes you too far.

When you feel that there are too many things draining your energy, it's time to pull back. Think about how to reduce some of your commitments and share your responsibilities. Get both your partner and your children involved in more of the 'doing' and less of the 'helping'.

It might seem as though a working mother has enough to do without always putting pen to paper to make lists — but it's often a useful way of clarifying what is happening to you and to find in which direction you want to be going. Try writing down the things that you think are stressing you. You'll probably find that there are both 'internal' and 'external' pressures.

Internal pressures

- worry
- guilt
- depression
- anxiety
- fear

External pressures

- financial problems
- job insecurity
- pressure of work
- family problems
- marital problems
- major life events such as illness or death
- small things, like losing the keys

Feeling in control

Feeling stressed is feeling that you aren't in control. And while you never will have control over events and situations, you can control how you feel about them. Stress is about how you perceive things, so if you can put those work pressures (the ones that you can't realistically control) into some kind of perspective and find a way of looking at them that isn't always negative, you'll feel better for it.

Try thinking of what you have to do as a challenge for you rather than a whole series of hurdles. See it as something positive to aim for and achieve. While this way of thinking mightn't come all that easily to begin with and you'll have to keep persuading yourself, it's worth it to find yourself in a better frame of mind at the end of your day. When you do feel overwhelmed or out of control because of the amount you have to do, try focusing on just one thing at a time.

> 'I force myself to relax in the evening and forget all my unfinished tasks.'

There are some things you can take practical steps towards solving or relieving. If you have financial pressures, for example, you can try cutting back weekly costs or taking on some overtime. You will also find that your energy levels and efficiency will increase if you can reduce the anxiety you have about your difficulties.

Take another look at your list and work out which of the things in your life that cause you stress you can eliminate altogether, realistically change, change your attitude to or accept by learning to relax about them.

How to cope

Practising relaxation techniques can make a huge difference to your daily life by giving your body a change of pace and your mind some space. Don't feel that you have to rush out and learn how to relax or panic that you won't have time. Even the simplest of practices, like taking a warm bath or using the deep breathing you learnt at childbirth classes, will give you physical, emotional and mental benefits.

It's a good idea, whether you are practising meditation, yoga or doing relaxation exercises, to schedule them into your day and have a regular time set aside that the rest of the family honours as your time. You can also look at some of your daily activities as opportunities to slow down your head and your body. Enjoy watering the garden, soaking in a warm bath or listening to peaceful music while you're ironing.

THE BENEFITS OF BREATHING

Bring this most natural and basic of practices into play whenever you find you are about to blow a fuse. When the children start fighting, you are caught in traffic on the way to childcare or your mother makes another dig at you because you are going to work when your child is sick — breathe.

Match your thoughts with your situation and you can use your breath for different purposes.

- When you need energy, think about your inhalations as being life-giving and invigorating.

- When you need calming, think about them as being strengthening.

- When you have trouble sleeping, think about letting go of the worries of the day as you breathe out.

- When you want to release tension, visualise the stress as falling away from your head and washing like water down your shoulders and over your back as you breathe out.

GIVE YOURSELF A BREAK

When you're at home, remind yourself that you don't always have to be on the go and give yourself permission just to sit quietly and do nothing. Have a cup of tea and put your feet up. Or pamper yourself with a foot massage or by painting your toenails and enjoy this as a symbol of time spent on yourself.

Make sure you take a proper break at work at lunchtime and go for a walk or do some other form of exercise like having a swim or going to the gym if you can. Make contact with other mothers in the workplace — it helps if you have someone to share your worries, troubles and triumphs with.

GOING ABOUT YOUR DAY

Have you found that you lie in bed at night with your fists clenched? As you go about your day, whether vacuuming, shopping or tasks at work, do you grip things really tightly and tense the muscles in your arms and neck? It's time to stop and look at how you are doing things, to let the tension wash away. Pay attention to some of your daily activities.

- When you're out shopping, see how lightly you can hold things without dropping them.

- When you carry a basket or a bag, make sure you don't tense your shoulders.

- Check your posture at work. When you sit at your desk, move forward in your chair and straighten your back. Place both feet flat on the floor because crossing your legs can restrict the flow of major arteries, especially if you cross them at the thighs.

- Loosen your grip on the telephone receiver.

- Don't hunch your shoulders when you are on the phone.

- If you work at a computer, remember to give your eyes, neck and arms a rest by taking regular breaks.

- Check your shoulders every so often to see if they are hunched. Open out your chest, pull your shoulders back and down and breathe deeply.

★ NECK TENSION RELEASE ★

The neck and shoulders are the area that most often suffers from tension. Here is a series of simple exercises you can do throughout the day to help relieve tightness.

- Drop your head to your chest and count to four. Return to the normal position.

- Turn your head as far to the right as you can, looking over your shoulder. Count to four and then return to the normal position.

- Drop your head back as far as it will comfortably go. Count to four and then return to the normal position.

- Turn your head as far to the left as you can, looking over your shoulder. Count to four and then return to the normal position.

- Roll your head from front, to right, to back, to left and then back the other way.

★ SHOULDER TENSION RELEASE ★

Sometimes you feel as though you are wearing your shoulders up around your ears. Here are two gentle exercises that will help put them back where they belong.

- Pull your shoulders right up to your ears and hold for the count of four. Slowly relax the muscles and lower your shoulders. Repeat four times.
- With your arms hanging loose by your sides, roll your shoulders and upper arms up and forwards in a circle four times. Then roll them up and backwards four times.

MASSAGING YOUR SHOULDERS

Try this self-massage for general relaxation or for tension headaches. It is best done after a hot bath and should always be done slowly and gently.

- While sitting, use one hand to massage the muscles of the opposite shoulder. Use the other hand to support the elbow of the massaging hand. Reach with your fingertips as far down your back as possible to the lower shoulder muscles.
- Knead the muscles by squeezing them between the fingers and the heel of the hand. You'll find that your hand slowly slides off. Repeat two or three times.
- Change sides and repeat the procedure.

If you wish, you can make your own massage oil by mixing two-thirds of a cup of cold-pressed virgin olive oil and one-third of a cup cold-pressed soya bean oil. For a general relaxation massage, add four drops of essential lavender oil. For a massage to ease tense muscles, add four drops of essential rosemary oil. Store the massage oil in a brown glass bottle which you can find at a chemist or health food store. You may need to invert the bottle to disperse the essential oil.

LAUGH A LITTLE MORE

'If you're too busy to see the funny things in your life, it's time to change your lifestyle.'

When you're tired and stressed, your life can be clouded with seriousness and the best remedy you'll find is to lighten up. Humour and laughter defuse stress and help give you perspective and balance. The therapeutic nature of humour is well known and you can so easily find it all around you when you live with a family. It's there in the simplest of things — take time out to watch your toddler negotiating life or pause to enjoy the antics of a family pet.

Humour also connects families. Think about it — aren't some of your fondest childhood memories the funny ones? At family get-togethers, isn't it always the funny family stories that are told?

One of the great things about having children around is that it's so easy to laugh with them. Just think about it:

- There's nothing they love more than when you act the fool. The sillier you are the more they'll roar.

- It gives you the perfect opportunity to be a kid again yourself — play.

- It gives you the chance to show your children that life can be fun.

- Watch comedies together and have a good laugh together.

- And don't forget to laugh at yourself.

EXERCISE

Exercise is both a reducer of stress and an energiser and is well worth the trouble it takes to fit it into your daily routine. Its almost magical qualities can improve your state of mind as well as being. Make sure, though, that you find something you like doing, or a few things that you can alternate, because if you don't enjoy doing the exercise you won't keep it up.

Another good reason to find something you like is to avoid giving yourself another burden and yet another source of guilt where you find yourself saying 'I should go to the gym...' Remember, too, that it doesn't matter how good you are at it or what anyone else may say or think. You are doing this for your own body and soul.

Sometimes it's difficult to find enough time to exercise but here are some suggestions.

- Think of ways to walk more; for example, park the car a little further away from work than you usually do.

- Use the stairs instead of the lift at work if you can.

- Arrange with a friend to go for a walk at lunchtime.

- Borrow an exercise video. Some have programs that only take 15 minutes.

- When doing household tasks, think of them as exercises. It may take a little longer to put things in cupboards if you are consciously stretching or bending your knees, but it will be good exercise.

- Have fun with your family while you exercise: go for bike rides, walk the dog or play ball in the park together.

A HEALTHY DIET

No mother needs to be told again the benefits of a good diet for all the family. You aren't, after all, deliberately going to fill yourself up with food that's bad for you — well, not really deliberately.

Take stock regularly and see where your (and your family's) eating habits are heading. It's easy to fill up the supermarket trolley with what everyone likes rather than what they need or is good for them. But if you try, you'll find it's not really so hard to steer the trolley away from the convenience foods and over to the fresh ones. Remember, too, that some of the simplest foods to prepare are the best for you.

CHAPTER 4

GUILT AND OTHER EMOTIONS

You feel guilty if you go to work, you feel guilty if you stay at home. You feel guilty if you do too much for your child and guilty if you don't do enough. If you're single you're guilty because you're not two people and you aren't providing a full family life. And if that doesn't make you feel bad enough, you can feel guilty about the fact that you aren't the perfect mother.

Full-time work, full-time guilt

You can rest assured that as a working mother you'll feel guilty at some stage in your life if not throughout it. You won't need a particular focus and nothing even has to go wrong. In fact, even when things are looking pretty damned good, you'll still feel guilty. Everything may seem okay now, but what will your child be like in later life? Will she have suffered because you went to work?

> 'If I could find a job that paid me well enough and allowed me to work only during school hours I'd leap at it. I'm not working full-time because I want to: the problem is that we need two full-time incomes to pay the mortgage and our bills. This makes it hard and when problems arise like the kids are sick then I feel even more guilty.'

Sometimes it doesn't take much: just a few words from your nearest and dearest can start the guilt snowballing. You may find that your own mother isn't past the odd gibe because, chances are, she stayed at home to care for you when you were young. You may discover your partner's hidden resentment because, despite the fact that you thought you were sharing the responsibility and the workload, when something goes wrong it's your fault.

Working mothers grow guilt buttons that everyone knows how to press. Well signposted, they say 'This is where it really hurts'. It's inevitable that when there's too much on your plate, your ability to respond instantly to the family's needs will diminish and, understandably, you'll feel bad about it. As a female in this society, you have probably grown up with the belief that the responsibility for the running of the home and family is yours, so, equally understandably, you'll find it difficult to refuse the responsibility simply because you are working as well.

The whole question, too, of what is best for your child is a minefield and weighs on your mind much of the time. And how are you expected to work things out when, in this constantly changing world, it would seem that even the 'experts' can't agree? Every few years the fashions in parenting change and there's yet another rash of theories and books.

There are those that believe that there are benefits in small children going to childcare and then there are those that believe that there are benefits in small children not going to childcare. The only thing that is certain is that you can't assume that there is one way of bringing up children that will suit all. As with so many aspects of your life, individual differences count for an enormous amount and what suits one family won't necessarily suit another. What is important is that if you, as a parent, feel comfortable and happy about what you are doing then that will flow on to your child.

Although feeling guilty about the quality of your mothering isn't the exclusive domain of mothers who work, when there is some difficulty, you can't help but wonder if it would be the same if you stayed at home. Remind yourself that all families have their problems and raising children is rarely smooth sailing. Also, everyone makes mistakes but yours isn't that you are a working mother.

Unfortunately there is a stereotype of a mother who is always available for her children, so, often, a working mother feels acutely that she is letting her child down. There is plenty to remind you that you aren't there for your child 100 per cent of the time and that you can't pick her up when school finishes, you can't go to all the school functions, and you can't do canteen duty regularly like some other mothers.

> 'I always feel guilty about not being a stay-at-home mum and I deal with it by giving my son as much affection and involvement as I can when I am with him.
> Then I feel guilty that I don't do enough of that either so I make sure that there are lots of other people around for him, like his grandmother, other relatives and friends.'

What to do about it

Telling a mother not to feel guilty is like telling a mother not to worry. There are some things you can do, though, to remove some of this burden.

Persuade yourself that you don't have time for negative feelings like guilt. If they are vague feelings, try to change them by reminding yourself of the positive aspects that your working brings to your life and to your child. Think of the things like interests for you outside the home, more independence for her, the increase in your self-esteem — and of course the money.

Try to deal directly with any specific areas of guilt. For example, if you feel guilty that you don't make enough time for your child, set aside an amount of time that you devote to her alone each day. If you feel guilty that you don't pay enough attention to her schoolwork, make sure you look at her homework every evening and talk to her about what she did that day.

Remind yourself you can only do your best and that includes doing the best for yourself. Being a happy and contented person will make you a better mother, even if you're a tired one. Feeling fulfilled and having high self-esteem make you a better role model for your child than a mother who is at home and unhappy (which you would be if you couldn't pay the bills).

Working mother guilt myths

MYTH NUMBER 1: GOOD MOTHERS STAY AT HOME
The idea that motherhood is an exclusive occupation is a recent one. In the past children were more easily integrated into mothers' working lives or were minded by siblings, relatives, neighbours or servants.

MYTH NUMBER 2: CHILDREN NEED THEIR MOTHERS
If you arrange good childcare there is no reason why your child shouldn't thrive. Children in childcare can have the benefit of educational input and stimulation as well as a wider social network.

MYTH NUMBER 3: HOW WILL SHE COPE?
Of course you'll wonder how your baby will survive in the outside world, but you'll find she'll gain a lot by learning to interact with other children and adults. She'll grow to be socially at ease, independent and self-confident.

MYTH NUMBER 4: SHE'LL GROW TO LOVE HER CARER MORE
The bond between mother and child isn't that easily replaced. It's good for her to grow to love and trust a number of people, not just you.

MYTH NUMBER 5: SHE'LL BE A LATCHKEY KID WHO GETS INTO TROUBLE
Being unsupervised doesn't mean she'll get into trouble. You'll find it's more likely she'll grow into the trust and responsibility you give her.

MYTH NUMBER 6: SHE'LL BE SHORT-CHANGED IN MY ATTENTION
This fear means that you tend to make every minute together count, which wouldn't be the case if you were at home with her all day.

MYTH NUMBER 7: THERE MUST BE SOMETHING WRONG WITH ME IF I WANT TO WORK
Liking the stimulation and satisfaction of working, the company of adults, the financial reward and self-respect doesn't add up to being a bad mother. Good fathers enjoy all those things too.

MYTH NUMBER 8: WHAT DO OTHER PEOPLE THINK OF ME?
Does it matter? If you are really worried about disapproval, ask some other working mothers what they think.

'I feel really lucky to have had a working mother. She was aware of the world. I think she supported me and encouraged me in a way that a mother who stayed at home couldn't have done. She was a great role model.'

Taking on too much

Girls are often conditioned to be the caretakers and to take responsibility for home and family. Now that you're a working mother, you are taking on more roles but you may not be relinquishing any. There are other aspects of girls' upbringing that contribute to the problem of taking on too much: some have been encouraged to be 'people pleasers' and find it hard to say 'no' and some have been taught to have unrealistic expectations of what they should accomplish and therefore put too many and too high demands on themselves.

'It's hell really, but what do you do? I'm a single parent and I have a mortgage to pay and I'm also a responsibility freak. I hate not to do my best and I know I put a lot of pressure on myself. I have to learn to let some of the responsibility go, but I just keep hoping a millionaire will come along and take me away from all of this.'

The problem for most of us is not just trying to do too many things but trying to do all of them too well. We don't need to strive for perfection in everything. You'll find that you don't have to put 100 per cent effort into all the things you do. This doesn't mean that you are learning to settle for less or letting your standards drop but only that a little less of your effort will still bring good results. Have high but realistic standards and you'll find that 80 per cent of your effort will do.

Not only can the compulsion to be perfect cause you major problems but it can run over into your expectations of your family as well. Remind yourself that it doesn't matter if they don't do something as well as you do, or even as well as you think they should, as long as they do it as well as they can.

Sometimes you can be your own worst enemy, so ease up on yourself a bit. It's okay to make mistakes, after all you're human, and you don't have to go all out in everything. At the same time, think about how you can reduce some of your commitments and share more of your responsibilities with your family.

Feeling inadequate

"I think I'm only just managing to stay "a page ahead of my pupils" as it were. It feels like a real treadmill — no time to take stock, no time to change — so I just try to do my best and tell myself it's okay to fail a fair bit.'

It would take a superwoman not to feel stressed living life at the pace of a working mother. There's the emotional side of things with your feelings ranging from the high of enjoying it all, to not thinking you are doing it well enough, through to times when it's completely overwhelming and out of control.

At times you will be filled with doubt — you don't know whether you are doing what you ought to be doing. You want to do what is best for your family but you aren't always certain what is right and what isn't.

You have been brought up to feel responsible for the care and wellbeing of your family and the problem is that when something goes wrong, instead of looking at the difficulty of the situation, you can so easily blame yourself. Mislaid notes, forgotten lunches and the state of the house are all your fault. You need to remind yourself that what you are doing and what you are trying to achieve in a day is hard work. Just because you feel it's hard doesn't mean that you are inadequate but simply that you have too much to do in too little time.

Resentment

Taking on more and more in your daily life and not giving anything up will inevitably make you feel resentful. Many working mothers don't share responsibility often enough and race around trying to do it all. Some assume that other family members will automatically pitch in without being asked and resent it if they don't. Others resent what seems to be an attitude that the family's contribution is 'help' rather than simply doing their share.

The problem with resentment and anger is that either you take it out on those around you or you turn it against yourself which can result in depression or a loss of self-esteem. But remember that you can't blame other people if you don't let them know what's going on or if you are putting their needs before your own.

Getting off the worry-go-round

'Instead of worrying, put your energy towards things that you value.'

What mother doesn't worry? It's in the job description, after all. What's important is being able to tell the difference between real concerns and unnecessary worry. There are times when you need to dwell on a problem in order to solve it but not if it mightn't ever happen. How many times have you worried about something and how you are going to handle it only to find that it didn't happen at all the way you thought it would?

There's no point in simply telling someone not to worry. There are, however, ways to stop yourself from being a worrywart which inevitably costs you time, energy and sleep. Worry can come from feeling responsible for things but sometimes they aren't even your responsibilities you're dwelling on.

Stop and think what your major concern is at the moment and ask yourself if there is anything you can do about it. How will you go about finding a solution? You are going to have to accept some things because they can't be changed and you'll have to persuade yourself that there's no point in your worrying about this. Try saying:

• I won't worry about this now.

• Will this matter to me in a week's time?

• Does this worry really warrant my time and energy?

• What are some of the things I can solve?

Often you'll find that you can be more stressed by the worry of what might happen than what actually is happening. It helps to keep in the present and take it day by day. Try to forget yesterday's guilt and stay away from tomorrow's fear and remind yourself each day of the small but simple things that have happened in your family and working life that have brought you pleasure.

It's okay to make mistakes

The only person who's expecting you to be perfect is you. Remind yourself that making mistakes is part and parcel of being human and look at them for what you can learn from them rather than regarding them as blots on your copybook.

Sometimes fear of making a mistake can even stop you from trying to do something. But, as they say, 'You don't know what you can't do until you try'. Think positively — actively believe in your abilities and, if you happen to get it wrong, your problem-solving abilities.

If you think you have failed at something, see it as an opportunity to stop and take stock. It's a chance to pause and reflect rather than continue in a hurly-burly fashion.

Be prepared for the highs and the lows

There's a real mix of emotions involved in being a working mother. There's the enormous satisfaction when everything's going well and you enjoy every facet of your life. Then, sometimes, a little anxiety or fear creeps in when you think what a balancing act it is. And sometimes it's totally overwhelming and you're probably better off not thinking about it at all and just going ahead.

> 'Sometimes I think "This is great — you've got it all". Other times I wish I could throw it all away and live alone on a desert island. I might sound like I'm a bit of an extremist with these highs and lows but it sure beats being bored.'

CHAPTER 5

THE PEOPLE IN YOUR LIFE

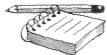

Okay, so you manage to get the food on the table, keep everyone's clothes relatively clean and put in a reasonable day's work. You're pretty sure you would recognise your husband if you passed him in the street but you can't remember your best friend's telephone number. Hold on a minute, this isn't how you want to live your life. You want to enjoy your family and friends.

Your relationships

Taking pleasure in the many things you do as a working mother is one of the great satisfactions of your life but what matters most are the people around you. When you're rushed and stressed you can so quickly forget that relationships require attention, even when they're not troubled. Whether it's with your children, your partner, your mother or a friend — your relationships need feeding a regular basis.

Given their importance, it's strange but it's not uncommon that you can easily neglect this part of your life until something goes wrong. You may recognise that what you feel you are constantly missing is time with the people you care about, and you keep saying that you'll catch up 'soon' but 'soon' never seems to come.

At the end of the day — even though it might be a long, hard day — surely caring for yourself, your family and those near and dear to you comes before all else.

Looking after you

Being a working mother isn't about making sacrifices. The days of the doormat are well and truly over. Whether working is what you really want or a choice you've made for practical reasons, you can still enjoy the immense satisfaction that such a full life can bring. In order to do this, though, you have to consider you and how you look after yourself.

How you feel about yourself — your self-confidence and self-esteem — has a large effect on how you go about your life, on your energy and on your family. If you have an 'I can do it' rather than an 'it's too hard' or a 'poor pitiful me' attitude, you'll find that you:

• rely on your own inner strength to get you back up when you fall down;

• become confident about your own resourcefulness and problem-solving skills;

• feel okay about asking for help when you need it;

• turn negatives into positives.

Being more assertive

How well you survive being a working mother depends on how assertive you are and on your ability to set limits on the amounts of time and energy you expend on the different aspects of your life. When you are more assertive your self-esteem improves and other people will also respect you more.

For many women it doesn't come all that easily but you can learn some simple techniques for being more assertive through courses or books. A local community health centre should be able to give you more information about courses and any large bookshop has a self-help section with a multitude of books. Different ones say different things to different people so it's worth browsing till you find one that speaks your language rather than just following someone else's recommendation.

> 'I can find time for my son and I can find time for my work. What I'm still working on is finding time for myself. But I figure two out of three ain't bad.'

Too often the last person a working mother thinks about is herself. Remind yourself that it's important:

• that you aren't manipulated by your children, partner, colleagues or relatives;

• that you don't feel you have to be perfect;

• that you take the time to restore your energy;

• that you learn to say 'no' every time saying 'yes' would stop you from doing what you feel you need to or want to do.

Give to yourself

Even when you have the support of a partner, there's a lot of giving out involved in being a working mother but you can't keep giving without getting something back. Apart from the fact that it isn't good for you — or for your children to grow up in such a situation — over time you will become resentful because no one is meeting your needs. While you can quite reasonably expect the support of those around you, it's up to you to look after yourself too.

'I'd always get home late and I'd feel frazzled and I'd stay that way until bedtime. Then I started jumping straight into a bubble bath when I got home. When my son was very small he'd sit on a chair and I'd read him a story. When he got older he'd do his homework. Now he can see what a difference my bath makes to me and he recognises it's my time and he lets me soak in peace.'

Plan some time that is for you alone. On a day-to-day basis it could be soaking in a bath, taking a walk or meditating. Swap nights out with your partner so you can go out with friends and leave him babysitting the kids. As well as your time alone together as a couple, it's important that you regularly have the opportunity to do something you enjoy. Spend time with other women friends, talking, seeing a film, or go to an exercise or yoga class. If you are a single mother, organise for your child or children to spend the night at their grandparents', their father's or a friend's place so you can have some space.

Talk to yourself

Your mind can be your best friend or your worst enemy. Some days it will help you achieve what you thought you couldn't and other days it will make you absolutely useless. The chatter going on inside your head becomes a part of your belief system so that if you're constantly hearing 'I can't cope' and 'I'm so tired', that's how you'll feel. Most of the time you won't even be aware of your negative self-talk because you're so used to it.

Sometimes, in order to keep up your energy levels and keep on top of all the 'to dos', you'll need to talk yourself into a positive frame of mind. You'll have to be on your guard and catch yourself when you're being negative in order to turn it around. Be prepared to keep at it and don't expect to change overnight, because you've had many years of conditioning.

Get support

Often one of the things a busy working mother doesn't have the time to maintain is one of the most vital — your support system. This can include your partner, family, friends, relatives, neighbours and your local and work community.

Both physical or emotional support will make your life easier during the tough times and it's not only a question of what other people can actually do for you. For many women it's enough just to know that someone is there should they be needed for help or just to talk to. Although it might seem as though there's no time or energy to foster and nurture your relationships with friends and neighbours, you'll find in the long run that they can be one of your most valuable assets.

You and your partner

Having children can be both uniting and divisive for you and your partner. While they bring an enormous amount of joy, children can also put the greatest strain on a relationship because there is a shortage of time and energy to complete all the jobs that they create and much less time for you as a couple.

Often you'll find that you disagree about what needs to be done and when. What stresses you isn't always that clear either, which means it's more difficult to deal with and, over time, becomes more potent. For example, while few men these days would actually declare themselves opposed to participating in the household work, often their lip-service exceeds their input. And while women want their partners to help, many still want to have control and the ultimate 'say' in how things around the home are done.

While it might take time and effort to work out what is going on and how you will deal with it, remind yourself of the long-term benefits for you and for your family. Your household will be happier if you aren't overtired and resentful and if your partner is more involved with the home life and his children.

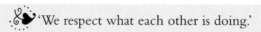 'We respect what each other is doing.'

TIME FOR EACH OTHER

When you are a working couple bringing up a family, the pressures of time are felt by you both. It's easy to start to take this most familiar of relationships for granted and for the warmth and romance to disappear.

In theory spouses make themselves available to each other but it doesn't always happen in practice. When your children are small you might have your time alone together after they are in bed, but as they get older and stay up later, this time diminishes.

While it might sound particularly unromantic, the thing to do is to schedule your time together. On a daily basis:

- take some time out together when you first get home so that you can reconnect — it might be only ten minutes;

- don't let your children interrupt this time — theirs comes later;

- talk if you want but don't have a competition about who had the worst day. If you don't feel like talking, just sit.

On a less frequent basis, plan time out together. The best-selling novelist Danielle Steel goes with her businessman husband to a house they own just down the road once a week. They spend every Thursday afternoon alone together at their cottage. While you might not be able to plan something quite so romantic or extravagant, there are more practical alternatives. Plan a dinner for two at your favourite restaurant, organise a bushwalk (without the kids) or come up with a surprise. It's wonderful to get home to find that someone else has already phoned the babysitter and made the theatre booking. Who knows? Perhaps he'll think to do it next time.

Your children

Your levels of stress and fatigue affect your parenting and it's not hard to feel as though you are all over the place. What matters most is to have clearly set out routines that you stick to and house rules that don't waver. When you're tired it might seem as though it's impossible to stand by them but it's worth drawing on your reserves because you'll find that once they're in place things will flow more smoothly on the home front.

MEAN IT WHEN YOU SAY 'NO'

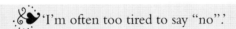 'I'm often too tired to say "no".'

From a very early age your children will work out your weak spots and where to aim when you're feeling down. They can become experts in manipulation.

What's important is that you continue to control your own feelings instead of letting your child control them. While it might take some resolve and some practice at keeping calm — which could be deep breathing that you can do in the privacy of your own bedroom — it will stand you in good stead in the years to come. When your child asks for something you don't want him to have:

- say 'no';

- instead of becoming angry when the request is repeated just keep saying 'no' quietly;

- practice a relaxation technique like breathing and focus on staying calm and centred while you continue to say 'no' to each request.

When you're a working mother you may overcompensate for not being there for your child. You may find yourself rushing around taking him places, buying him things and catering to his whims in a desperate attempt to make up for your dreadful neglect during the working week. Instead of acting on impulse, weigh up whether the demands are reasonable or if there is another way for his needs to be met and him to pursue his own interests.

> 'I spend the weekends on the road driving my children from A to B and back again. My wallet's always empty and my credit cards full because I keep buying them things to make them happy. I feel that physically and materially I'm trying to compensate for the fact that I've chosen to work.'

Tips for a working mother

While they say parenting isn't for the faint-hearted, it certainly doesn't help being a fatigued working mother. These tips might help you keep clear-headed and on track:

• Grade the responsibilities and challenges you give to your children as they grow up.

• Keep rules to a minimum so that they count.

• State the rules in a positive way.

• Say 'yes' as often as you can: then when you say 'no' it'll have more impact.

• Above all, try to be consistent.

TEACH SELF-HELP

It's very easy to get into the habit of doing things for your family. It makes them happy, it makes you happy. Often, too, as you rush around you don't notice that your child is growing up and is now capable of doing more for himself.

You think you will make it up to all the family for not being permanently 'available' if you do more for them. Add to this your lack of time and energy and it seems much simpler and faster just to do something yourself rather than try to coax them into it or put up with an unsatisfactory result.

It isn't good for any of you to live like this, so think about how you can get your child to do more for himself. Think about what you can do to make your home more user-friendly. How can you plan the kitchen, for instance, so that there's more that he can do for himself? What kitchen appliances, like a microwave or a jaffle iron, would mean that he could make his own after-school snacks or weekend lunches for the family?

Of course, as your child grows up your expectations of him and his responsibilities will change. There are some general points to keep in mind.

• When your child expresses interest in doing things for himself, let him try even if it takes longer or makes a mess.

- Encourage him to make decisions for himself — from how much shampoo to use to when he feels he is ready to catch a train by himself.

- Be positive when he takes the initiative, even if he gets it wrong.

- Give him positive feedback for being careful and responsible.

Start them early

You will all be better off if you get your child to do things for himself from an early age. For example, he should learn to get dressed and undressed, wash himself and clean his own teeth as soon as he is able. Unfortunately not all children will be keen to do so and will try to get you to do it for as long as possible. In the interests of time now you'll sometimes feel like giving in but your perseverance is worth it in the long run.

By the time a child turns three he should be pretty well able to dress himself, although he will still need help with some things. Obviously, pulling on a pair of shorts is easier than tying shoelaces.

Teaching a child to dress himself is a long-term project but if you start when he is a toddler you are preparing him well. Try these dressing tips.

- Buy clothes that are easy to put on and take off, such as shoes with Velcro rather than laces and T-shirts rather than shirts with buttons.

- Make sure his clothes are laid out for the morning.

- Don't allow any distractions like watching TV while dressing.

- Praise him for his efforts.

- Only give help when it's needed.

- Make sure he has plenty of time to get dressed — tempers will fray when you're racing the clock and things are bound to go wrong.

If you start early and work on it, by the time he is 10 he'll be washing his own clothes, ironing them at 12 and buying them with his own clothing budget at 16.

REGULAR RESPONSIBILITIES

Decide on a few regular responsibilities that your child can learn to regard as his own. He will benefit from the sense of accomplishment as he becomes more proficient at them and it will also help you out.

Getting into the habit early on of packing his own school bag will not only help him become more organised but he'll know what he's put in it. To start with, you might need to be there and hand him the things while he puts them in and then get him to gradually take responsibility for the whole procedure.

A child learning to pack his own bag when he goes away on holidays and to camps has more advantages than just your not having to do it. It means he knows what he has in the bag and you can avoid any complaints about not packing the right shirt. It gives him an opportunity to pack what he likes to wear and what he thinks he'll use. When he's small you can put out the clothes for him to pack.

Communicating

With the time pressures of your lifestyle you can lose some of the opportunities to communicate with your family and friends. It may seem artificial to have to plot talking time but it's a vital element of family life that shouldn't be neglected. Not only does it give you the chance to find out what's happening with the members of your family but it teaches your children valuable communication skills.

Turn your evening meal into your important time together when you all have the chance to sit down quietly and communicate with each other and your child has the opportunity to practise social skills. It doesn't mean your child can't escape to a friend's house for the night or that you can't go out, but that when you are all at home together it's a given that you observe this evening ritual.

Take it in turns to invite other families over to share your evening meal with the understanding that it's an early night and simple fare. It takes the pressure off entertaining and gives you the opportunity to catch up more often.

Nurturing your friends

'I find that I see much less of my friends than I would like to but I know that they are there. I'm always hoping that things will improve on the work front and that I'll have more time but then again I'm also doing a part-time degree. Perhaps I should just accept that this is the way it'll always be.'

The list of benefits in having a good friend is endless. It's great to have someone who understands without your saying anything, who offers help before you ask and always endeavours to be there when you need a cup of coffee and a 'Life stinks' conversation. Even if you don't get to see them all that often in your hectic schedule, you know that they're there in the background.

Having friends in the same boat can be of enormous support. Not only do you have interests in common, you are in a position to commiserate and you can call on each other for practical help, but it also means you don't have to explain why it has been so long since they heard from you. It's also not too hard to organise social activities, like family picnics, where everyone brings their own fare and weekend lunches where children have their playmates as well.

On the other hand, you can run into the risk of trying to be all things to all people when it comes to your friends and find that you end up not being anything to anyone. Take a look at the people that matter and decide how you will show them that you care. It doesn't have to be anything material but could be something precious nevertheless, like some of your time. Plan ahead and book a Saturday afternoon with a close friend to go out for a coffee and chew the fat. Organise a simple celebration for her birthday.

Every now and then it's important to stop and have a close look at your friendships to see what they do for you, which doesn't mean whether the individual lends a helping hand but what he or she does for the way you feel. Some people drain energy either through their emotional demands, through their negativity or because they undermine you. If you find that someone has a toxic effect on you, then you'll need to think about whether you want to try to change the dynamics of an unsupportive relationship or whether you just have to let it go.

CHAPTER 6

WHEN YOU'RE SINGLE

While the life of a working mother is hard, the life of a single working mother can be a recipe for madness. Double doses of guilt and responsibility, lashings of fatigue, half the amount of money, a dash of loneliness, mixed with a little resentment (optional). Preferably shaken not stirred.

You're on your own

While working mothers with partners and single working mothers face largely the same problems and dilemmas, the single working mother faces them alone. The hardest thing about being a single working mother is that there is no one there to help you — whether it's to slip out to buy a litre of milk or to call on if you do have to stay back for a vital meeting.

If you don't do it, it doesn't get done. You can't call on someone else when you're too tired to argue or to say 'no' and you can't hand over a problem indicating that 'This one's yours'.

You have total responsibility for the family, for the running of the household and for the finances, so the burden can start to weigh heavily. On top of that, you have no choice but to work to support your family, and while your friends can enjoy the benefits of two incomes, you often struggle to survive on one.

It's a question not only of the physical support but of the emotional support. You won't get it, and can't expect it, from small children. You may long for someone who'll listen to the details of your day and remind you that the world will look a better place in the morning. From the early hours until late at night you feel you are giving out and there's no one there to give back. It's not to say that friends and family can't be supportive but it makes a difference having someone who's emotionally close to you and on-site, who'll understand your silliest of concerns as well as the major family dramas.

Practical problems

Being on your own means that you are the one who has to take your baby to childcare and your child to school and pick them up; you don't have someone to fall back on when either you or your child is sick; and if you want to go out, you have to hire a babysitter which might well break the bank.

Rather than feeling overwhelmed by the fact that you have to do it all, think about solutions.

• Take turns with someone who lives close by to drop children at school or childcare.

• Make arrangements with a friend to be backup for each other in emergencies.

• Arrange to pick up another child one day a week in return for that being done for you. It can be well worth it to have one day when you don't have to rush to a carer or centre.

• Swap babysitting. When children are small you can move them about quite easily at night without disturbing their sleep. As they get older you might need to think about having them stay overnight. Most children feel quite comfortable with this if they get used to it from an early age, especially when they have a friend to wake up to.

Father's involvement

Of course it's going to be a help to you if your child's father is an actively involved parent. Obviously, access arrangements and relationships with ex-partners vary considerably but it will make a great difference to you if you feel you can rely on him to take some of the load.

Some parents share school holiday arrangements, some fathers will help out with babysitting during the week in order to give you some time off to go to an exercise class or catch up with friends, and some will make sure they are always there for the regular weekend sporting activity. On weekends it can be great help to have someone to share the chauffeuring, particularly when you have more than one child with activities to get to.

> 'I know it's not always easy and it took us a lot of hard work to get there but I think it's really important to try to get on with your ex-husband. While he might have been a not-so-hot husband, he's a great father and our children really benefit from our getting on well. He sees them a couple of times a week, which gives me a very welcome break as well as being terrific for the kids.'

Asking for help

Any reluctance you might feel about asking for help will quickly disappear when you find how eager people are to give you assistance. Most people are only too glad to do something for their neighbours and friends, especially those who are aware of the difficulties facing single working mothers.

Often the most difficult part of asking for someone's help is getting up the courage. After that it's all downhill and let's face it — the worst that can happen is that they'll say 'no' and you'll have to try someone else. If you're worried that you are imposing on people, spread your requests for help around and don't put too many demands on any one person or family. Also make a conscious effort to repay any favours you ask for; for example, if you get someone to pick your daughter up from school one day, offer to pick theirs up the next.

DON'T KEEP QUIET

You'll also find that just letting other people know your situation will give them the opportunity to help and support you without you having to ask directly. Staff in childcare centres and schools have seen many children from single-parent families come through their doors and they can offer your child a more supportive environment if they understand the situation. For example, small children are always busy working out their family relationships, which can be confusing or upsetting for a child whose parents have separated. If the carer or teacher understands this, then he or she can deal with it in an appropriate manner. When the class talk about their families, the teacher can use this as an opportunity to look beyond the mother, father and children family to one that may include grandparents or stepbrothers and stepsisters.

Take special care of yourself

Because you're a single parent you need to stay as fit, healthy and happy as you possibly can. Take special care of yourself in the absence of a loving partner. Make sure you find time and space for yourself, pay attention to your needs and nurture yourself. You can easily become the forgotten one.

Try to organise regular time off. Whether it means asking your child's father, asking a grandparent or paying a babysitter, you'll need some time when you don't have to think about being a parent. It's particularly important for you because you go it alone the rest of the time.

When you can afford it, buy yourself treats like a bunch of flowers instead of spending the money on something sensible. It can become a very serious business being a single working mother and there aren't many people around you who are in a position to encourage you to lighten up a little or be a little more reckless.

> 'I treat myself to a massage once a month. It does me the world of good to have someone paying me all that attention for an hour and it's also nice to be touched — other than by small sticky fingers.'

Your support systems

All working mothers need to develop support systems but you will need to be more conscious of yours. You need to think not only of what happens when your child is sick but of what happens when you are sick and there's no partner to take over. Is there someone you can call on to take the children to school?

Think about support systems in terms of how they will benefit your child as well. You can widen her circle of friends, both adults and peers, and help her to feel a part of a larger 'family' or network. You can't possibly be all things to her and this will give her the opportunity to develop different relationships that will help give her security and confidence.

Contact with family and friends — even if you have to go out and make them first — will help you and your child feel less isolated and less alone. It will also give you a break from each other's company. Even if you are visiting together, it breaks the dynamic of just you and your child.

When you start to look around a bit, you'll discover that it isn't hard to find other single working parents who are also eager for a bit of adult company. You might have to call on your courage to introduce yourself at a school function but you'll find that you rarely get a rebuff from another single parent. If you do have difficulty meeting people in your situation, try contacting groups like Parents Without Partners for a bit of moral support.

Avoid the negatives

Some people will make it quite clear that they feel sorry for you. When this happens, don't fall into the trap of self-pity but rather take it as an opportunity to show them that there is no reason for you to be pitied. You are in much the same situation as thousands of women and they are managing just fine, so there's no reason you won't too.

If they are determined to dwell on the fact that what you are doing is hard work, it might be time to move on to more positive people. It helps to have encouragement rather than feel you are being dragged down.

Double doses of guilt

Like other working mothers you'll probably feel guilty from time to time about what you aren't giving your children, but as a single working mother, it's easy to convince yourself that it's twice as bad. After all, you're only one person and you can't be everything to everyone and you can't be in all places at once. Who'll go and kick the football in the park on the weekend if you don't feel like it and who'll go to the school concert if you can't?

At times you'll feel bad because you can't provide your child with a real family life and, more often than not, you can't give her the same material things that two incomes can buy.

Remind yourself that you don't have to give twice as much to compensate for your being a single working parent. The very best that you can give her is a parent who feels good about herself and, more often than not, your working will contribute to this.

It's not too hard to find practical solutions to most of the areas that you could see as problems. You'll also need to keep reminding yourself of the positive aspects of single parenthood and your situation. If you don't want to go and kick the football, perhaps it will encourage your child to go and find a friend in the neighbourhood who does, or to think of something that you will enjoy doing together. If you can't make this school concert, you can plan ahead to make sure you get to the next one.

Remember the positives

When you start to fall apart and wonder why you ended up on your own and think about what a mess you've got yourself into, remind yourself that it is better than being in an unhappy relationship, for both you and your child. Not only would your self-esteem suffer if you were stuck in a miserable marriage but your child wouldn't have the benefit of the role model of a happy parent.

During the difficulties of separation, use your work to give you feelings of confidence and contribute to your self-esteem. You may even be lucky enough to have work colleagues who support you. Work also gives you time and space away from family and home where your current troubles lie.

Often a marriage with major problems will sap your energy because of the stress it creates. So in spite of what you might think, you probably aren't any worse off in terms of tiredness. While you might have to work a lot harder, it's positive work with positive outcomes.

Being on your own, you can create your own rules for the household and you won't have to make huge compromises. Many single mothers find they can manage to run a house more smoothly without a partner, sticking to their own routines and schedules. It's also said that a woman's workload generally increases more when she takes a partner than when she has children, so perhaps you are better off in some ways than other women in relationships.

'I like not having to negotiate any more and being able to make my own decisions about what we'll do and how we'll do it. My husband and I were always at loggerheads about even the simple things like how the table should be set. And that was before we even got to how we approached parenting. It leaves me with energy for more positive things.'

Sometimes, too, there is an advantage because you are quite clearly on your own. Some women with partners feel they carry many of the family and financial responsibilities without any real assistance from their partners and without any recognition. At least you are in a position where others can openly admire you for your achievements and you can congratulate yourself on what you do single-handed.

'When I look at a lot of couples around me I start to think that I am better off in lots of ways. Sure, it would be nice to have some support and some physical help — if he were that kind of guy but many of them aren't. I am thankful I only have to look after my daughter and myself.'

Many single working mothers talk about the wonderful relationships they develop with their children. In the absence of a partner, close friendships often grow along with the trust and sense of responsibility mother and child have towards each other.

'My child and I are very close and well tuned to each other's moods, which I regard as a good thing because it shows some sensitivity. We have been on our own together for ten years now, and while I don't think it would have been impossible for us to grow this close if I had a partner, I do think it would have been more difficult.'

CHAPTER 7

WHO'S DOING THE HOUSEWORK?

Those small furry things have started to multiply in the bottom of the fridge again and someone's threatening to visit, which means a major spring-clean. You shout and scream trying to persuade the rest of the family that things are in a mess and there's work to be done. Then when they do get around to helping, you begin to wish you'd done it yourself.

The truth about housework

'If the house looks better than you do, then you've got it all wrong.'

Let's face it, housework isn't anyone's favourite pastime. While there's the odd cleanliness freak out there, few people have a passion for polishing. And apart from being the thing that no one really wants to do, it can also bring out the worst in people — bickering, stalling and downright dirty play. Arguments about housework, or the lack of it, tend to be fiercely emotional and in no time you become an 'old nag' and you're living with a bunch of 'slobs'.

But of course there's housework and there's very ugly housework too. There are the things that we are all reasonably happy to do — like hanging the washing on the line. But while pegging may be a strangely simple and satisfying process, who in their right mind is going to jump at scrubbing the kitchen floor or cleaning the toilet?

Then there are the conspicuous jobs that can give you a great sense of reward — the ones you can get a round of applause for if you're so inclined. Many men seem to excel at these tasks and can manage to draw a crowd and some amazement by simply saying: 'Look at all this shopping I've done and the bargains I've bought. Can you believe I managed to get 30 air fresheners for only $20?'

'Don't do any housework at a time you can't be seen doing it.'

And the inconspicuous tasks that mothers are so familiar with, like scrubbing the ingrained grime from the inside rim of the favourite baseball cap. You get no Brownie points for that and you have to do it in the dead of night because it's the only time you can get it off the boy's head.

Facing facts

'We muddle through. We'll certainly never win the Good Housekeeping Award and I'm not sure that we make good role models for our son, although he does keep his own room tidy. Housework never was a great love of mine and it doesn't much matter to me that it's the thing that slips the most.'

While no one wants the housework to take the front seat we all recognise that a certain amount is essential. Remind yourself that it doesn't deserve the emotional energy that it usually absorbs and that what you are looking for is a way of getting the housework done (especially all those really dreadful 'have-to-be-dones') with the least amount of friction.

As it's an integral part of the running of the home, housework is an area that a mother generally sees as her responsibility whether she is in the paid workforce or not. So, often, you'll find that if you aren't the one doing it, you are the one urging other family members to action.

'Sometimes the battle to get someone to do it is more energy-sapping than if I do it myself.'

Look at all the shopping I've done!

While many men share the responsibility, some seem to be getting away with as little as they can. This is not to suggest that there's anything malicious going on, it's just that they haven't been brought up to see it as a part of their workload. Often, too, some of those with the best intentions still need a little training and this can prove to be a pretty tiring exercise in itself.

Many couples find that they are involved in a lot of negotiation and compromise about housework at the same time they're adapting to the changed situation of being a family with two working parents.

'My husband does more of the housework than I do because he's so fussy and I don't do a good enough job. He's obsessed about it and dusts and vacuums all the time. I'd prefer to be more relaxed about how we live but I can't complain really.'

In a household run by two parents who work it shouldn't be so much a question of who does the housework but of who does which jobs. Some family homes run smoothly without chore allocation but most, especially those with older children, benefit from having job descriptions so the tasks are distributed fairly and everyone knows what they should be doing without having to be reminded. With housework, it really is a case of being organised and efficient so you can save time, energy and despair — either in the actual doing or in seeing that it gets done. Think about purchasing whatever labour-saving devices, such as a dishwasher, that can help you around the home. Microwaves are not only useful for their speed but can be used by older children to make snacks and prepare meals.

'It's pretty well organised now and things run fairly smoothly — unless I am sick or unusually busy with work. Then everything falls apart and all hell breaks loose. Even though my husband does his share, and now that the kids are older they do theirs, it still seems to be up to me to be the one to organise and direct.'

The situation changes

Sometimes after having a child, you'll find you need to redistribute household chores because what has worked for you as a couple won't necessarily work for you now that you have the needs of an extra (helpless) person to fit into your busy schedule. You'll find, too, that your housework strategies will need revising over time as your children grow or your work situations change.

Often, too, your expectations of how you and your partner will share the responsibilities for housework after you've had a child won't match the reality. In this case you are going to have to either find a way to solve your differences or change your expectations. Otherwise, you will find yourself living a life of resentment.

Simplify your living

Don't make housework any harder than it needs to be. Take a good look around and work out what you can do to streamline your living. One of the most practical solutions is to have adequate storage space in your home so that everything has its own place and can be put away quickly and easily. Make sure that your child's room is user-friendly and that he can reach and use his storage spaces easily.

Think carefully about what you do now and what you could eliminate from your list of chores. You might try putting the clothes in the drier for a few minutes instead of ironing them and, say, not ironing tea towels at all. Even if the changes appear to be very small, you'll find that they'll gradually add up and start to make a difference. Ease up a bit — if you are crazy enough to think the floor needs vacuuming four times a week, try two and see if you can live with it. Then one.

Eliminate objects as well as tasks. A cluttered home is likely to become messy and is more difficult to clean. Be ruthless and get rid of things you are hanging on to that you really wouldn't miss. Have regular family spring-cleans so that all of you know what's in your cupboards and whether it needs to be kept.

'I clean one room at a time thoroughly and keep the others tidy. If I have one major clean–up every couple of weeks and do the little bits and pieces each day, it keeps the house pretty well under control.'

Here are some time-saving hints you may find useful.

- Get everyone to empty the pockets of their own dirty laundry, checking for tissues, lollies and notes.

- Don't bother to sort clothes into colours for washing but get the family to throw them straight into the machine. When it's full, do a cold wash so colours won't run.

- Do a load of washing each night so it's ready to hang out first thing next morning.

- Fold and put away the washing every day so there are no last-minute dramas when the cupboards are bare.

- Do a little ironing each day to keep in control of the basket.

- As soon as your child is old enough, get him to put away his own washing so he knows where everything is. You'll have to learn to shut your eyes for awhile when he crams a freshly ironed shirt into a drawer, but when he asks the eternal question 'Where's my...?' you can blithely say 'I don't know, you put it away'.

- Put clothes in the drier for a few minutes to save ironing.

Letting go

You may think that what you want is to find a way of doing a minimum of housework yourself but you may not be sending out those signals. Because it has traditionally been a woman's domain and you have grown up believing housework is your responsibility, you might have to learn to let go a little in order to take up other responsibilities in your life.

Though you may not mind all that much bringing the clean washing in, if you are always the one to do it, it leaves you less time for other things. Furthermore, the family won't benefit from being cooperative and you won't lighten your load.

Doing less of the work, however, means letting go of the control. You can't reasonably complain about other family members not contributing if you won't let them. You will need to consciously start getting them involved. More than likely it's a retraining process for all of you — they aren't going to leap at the opportunity to do housework and you have to start to think about how to get them to do it — without nagging.

Letting go can mean not being too fastidious about the way you live. After all, what you need is a reasonable degree of comfort and cleanliness and not necessarily a home that is always spick and span. Letting go also means being happy with someone else's work even if you don't think they've done it as well as you could, and remembering to encourage and not criticise when they've done it.

> 'Allow them to make mistakes. You do.'

This is hard for many women because the other side of it is that what you think is an untidy or dirty home can make you feel miserable. Part of what's involved is changing your way of thinking and learning to place priorities on other things such as time spent together with your children and partner rather than having your home as neat as a pin. You'll also have to learn to worry less about what other people think of your housekeeping standards.

> 'What motivates me most to clean the house is to invite people over, so I try to do it regularly. The rest of the time I'd rather spend resting, being with my daughter and generally enjoying myself.'

Apart from easing up on your overall housekeeping standards, you may have to let go of a little of the detail. Many of us have our own idiosyncrasies and bugbears but, at the end of the day, does it really matter that the socks aren't hanging in pairs on the line?

> 'I always end up doing it anyway.'

Whatever you do, don't play the martyr and say 'I'll do it' because nine times out of ten, they'll let you. The only one who will suffer in this situation is you, as your workload, resentment and anger grow.

Sometimes you might find that you are unconsciously sabotaging your family's housework because they don't do it your way. Make sure that you aren't:

- telling them how to do it unless you are teaching them for the first time;
- choosing to do it yourself because you don't like the way they do it;
- redoing it when they've finished.

It's time to loosen up and let them get on with the job.

Sharing the load

When you start to divide the tasks among the family members, you will begin to share the load. In order to change both their habits and yours you'll need to sit down and talk about it — about who's going to do what and when.

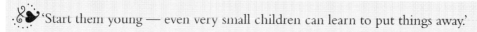 'Start them young — even very small children can learn to put things away.'

Obviously your expectations of what your child can contribute will change as he grows older, but you can start training him from quite an early age. A very small child can learn to put things away when he's finished with them and from about eight years of age you can have him vacuuming and doing the dishes. For a while you'll run the risk of not being able to find anything when he's put the groceries away, or having to mop the kitchen after he's done the washing-up, but you'll get used to it. Children have a knack of turning a chore into a game and the length of time it takes will seem ridiculous, but tell yourself that he's getting it done, it's just that he does it differently.

'I had to learn to ignore the bubbles floating to the floor and the kitchen looking like a swamp after his first attempts at washing-up. Food was still stuck to the plates. It was all a ploy because he thought if he did a bad job I wouldn't get him to do it again. It helped to turn a blind eye and he did get it right eventually.'

CHORES FOR SMALL CHILDREN

You can expect your child to do different tasks around the home at different ages. Remember to praise him for his efforts.

From about the age of two, you could teach him to:

- put away his own clothes and toys;
- water plants in the garden;
- carry things to and from the table;
- scrub potatoes;
- collect herbs from the garden.

From about the age of three, you could teach him to:

• make his own bed — especially if he has a doona instead of sheets and blankets;

• feed pets;

• water house plants;

• help with the washing-up — but not crystal glasses;

• measure ingredients for recipes and stir them together.

LET THEM LOOK AFTER THEMSELVES

Keep reminding yourself that you aren't there to pick up after other people. If your son has a drink and kicks off his shoes, then he has to put the cup and the shoes away when he's finished. All the family (including you) have to get used to the idea that they aren't there to 'help' you clean up their messes but that they're there to clean up their own.

A good habit for all the members of the family to develop is to put away their belongings and tidy up each evening before going to bed. There will be fewer hassles in the morning and you'll all have a fresh start to the day. Also, if they put it away, then theoretically they'll know where it is, and if they don't, they can't blame you.

Not only is it beneficial for the family as a whole for the various members to cooperate with housework but it's good for your children as individuals. It will help them to:

• develop a sense of responsibility;

• feel a sense of satisfaction in completing tasks, developing skills and learning perseverance;

• develop a sense of teamwork;

• understand the value of work and that it is an important ingredient of life;

• learn self-discipline and commitment;

• cooperate with others in other relationships in the future.

It's a good idea to have some basic house rules to keep things straight. A work-before-play rule can ensure that tasks get finished. Another rule might be that everyone — including you — has to pick up and clean up after themselves. And just as soon as they're old enough, each child has the responsibility of tidying his or her own room.

You might want to post chore charts on the noticeboard, making it clear who has to do what. You could encourage smaller children with stickers or stars when the chores are accomplished.

TAKE THE TIME TO TRAIN

When something has become second nature to you, it's easy to forget that it's a new skill to someone else. It's also easy to assume that everyone knows how to do housework. Call on your patience and take the time to tell your partner and your children any useful tips you have developed over the years as you've gone about the household chores.

Remember to do this in a positive way: encourage, don't criticise. You also must be prepared to let them develop their own skills and their own ways of doing things.

When you are really pushed for time and your child is small, it's very tempting to do things for him rather than go through the painstaking process of teaching him to do it for himself. You'll need to keep pulling yourself up on this one and reminding yourself that you aren't doing him or yourself any favours if you postpone his learning.

NAGGING DOESN'T WORK

Nobody likes being nagged. The members of your family are no exception and you can be assured that the more you nag the more they'll stall. The more they stall the more angry you'll become. Once you have established who is to do what, let them do it in their own way. Usually, if it takes 15 minutes rather than 5, that's okay. If it's done tomorrow instead of today, that's also usually okay. As long as they fulfil their obligations within a reasonable time frame, leave them be to work at their own pace in their own way. It probably isn't crucial that a child's bedroom is perfectly organised as long as it has a semblance of order. Remember, you aren't always right and they aren't always wrong.

Recognise that you'll have a range of different personalities in the family who will have quite different ways of going about things. Some will want to please, some would rather direct than be directed, and some are just plain stubborn. You'll find that your family will listen to you more easily if you lighten up, and your requests may have more effect if they're humorous or, with younger children, you make a game of it.

'I really only did it because I had run out of other tactics and never dreamt it would work so well. I got so fed up with my family not doing their bit around the house that I stopped doing anything too. I left dirty clothes on the floor, clean clothes in the ironing basket and, after a few days, they had got the message!'

Housework can be such an emotional issue that any difficulties can quickly flare up into a full-scale war. Try these general guidelines for negotiating a win-win situation when it comes to housework.

- Don't expect other people to anticipate what you want or to understand if you have a problem. State as clearly as you can what the difficulty is.

- Be specific and stay relevant — talk only about the particular problem at hand and don't go off on other tangents.

- Stay in the present with any particular issue: don't say things like 'You always...';

- Speak to the person in an appropriate manner — don't issue orders to your partner but be authoritative with your children;

- Always keep in mind the other person's self-image and don't undermine it — don't say things like 'You don't care about anyone else but yourself' or 'You're hopeless';

- Avoid personal remarks like 'You're a slob'.

REWARDS AND INCENTIVES

Of course there'll be times when the last thing that your child wants is to act as a part of a team and he'll go out of his way to resist. Also, there'll be times when he feels overtired and overworked just as you do.

There's no harm in rewarding for work well done. It can turn into a problem if a child expects to be rewarded for doing all his required daily chores but there's no reason for you all not to benefit when you have all contributed to a smooth-running week. Going out to eat on the weekend or hiring some videos could be a family treat.

You might consider nonmaterial rewards, such as reading a story, on a daily basis when all the work is done, or material rewards, such as money, for extra tasks like washing the car or mowing the lawn. Of course, the other side of it is that you can dock pocket money or restrict watching television if tasks aren't carried out.

You might want to strike deals like 'When you've done this we'll go bike-riding' or 'You can't have a friend over till you've tidied your room'. The immediate prospect of doing something you like can be the greatest incentive of all.

If there are tasks that everyone hates doing, like the vacuuming, you might want to pay one of the older children to do it. It will give him a sense of achievement and satisfaction and it also gives him the opportunity to learn that he can be rewarded for his efforts.

Charting the unknown

The thing about housework is that so much of it goes unnoticed unless you are the one doing it. In order for everyone (including you) to realise what's involved in running the household it's a good idea to make a list of the tasks. (You'll find a chore chart below that will make a good starting point.)

Performing the tasks doesn't necessarily have to be regimented but having a list to work to takes the responsibility of telling everyone what needs to be done away from you. This means you won't find yourself in the awful position of begging for their help or becoming a hideous nag. Undoubtedly they'll feel better, too, if they aren't being nagged or made the butt of verbal abuse.

Make several copies of this chart. Fill in the initials of the person to do the chore for that day of the week. Stick it on

	MON	TUES	WED
MEALS			
Breakfast			
Washing up			
Making lunches			
Dinner			
Washing up			
DAILY CHORES			
Making beds			
Tidying			
CLEANING			
Vacuuming			
Dusting			
Mopping floors			
Bathroom			
Kitchen			
WASHING			
Putting it out			
Taking it in			
Ironing			
Putting clean clothes			
away			
SHOPPING			
Major grocery shop			
Putting groceries away			
Keeping up supply of			
basics like milk and bread			
SMALL CHILDREN			
Bathing			
Dressing			
Feeding			
Packing their bags			
OUTDOORS			
Feeding pets			
Walking the dog			
Watering plants			

CHART ★

THURS	FRI	SAT	SUN

The positives of housework

If the thought of housework always fills you with a sense of dread, try turning around your way of thinking. Focusing on simple tasks can bring you balance. See them as a time to switch off from all the demands and as a chance to change pace. Setting aside a small amount of time for ironing each day means that the basket stays under control and you have the opportunity to quieten your mind, daydream and listen to peaceful music. Regard it as a relaxing exercise.

Some household chores are also physical activity — bending and stretching muscles that you mightn't usually stretch in the course of your working day. Remind yourself that in times gone by a typical day for most people was filled with a range of activities that kept their bodies strong and supple. It also helped keep them free of stress and anxiety.

Paid help

'My advice to any working mother is to get a cleaner as soon as you can afford it. We only have someone come once a fortnight but it really makes a difference to us all.'

Many working families buy what help they can. If and when you can afford it, think seriously about paying someone to clean your house. Consider your options when making the decision. Employing someone once a fortnight may be enough to get you through or perhaps a big clean every three months by a contract cleaner might suit you better.

However you manage it, it will give all the family more free time and will take away a major cause of friction on the home front. If you're a bit of a puritan and think hard work's good for you, you'll find that there are still plenty of daily chores that can keep you all occupied.

To be sure, sometimes hiring someone to do the cleaning can cause even more anxiety. Make sure:

• you aren't cleaning up for the cleaner;

• you're getting what you want and need;

• you don't spend an hour or two rearranging her rearrangements — say something!;

• you aren't frightened to say when it's not clean enough.

CHAPTER 8

YOUR WORK

Y ou find that your mind is always racing. In the middle of a budget meeting you suddenly remember that you have to book your child into vacation care; when you're standing in the supermarket queue you realise you left something out of a report. While it might feel good to change gear between work and home, the engine never stops.

Going back to work

Going back to work can be difficult for a number of reasons. Settling into a new regime is always hard; and then there's the worry about your baby, the guilt about not staying at home, the necessity to become organised in a different way, the adjustment to not having any time to yourself, as well as an overwhelming tiredness.

Some women are able to arrange to start at a job on a part-time basis, which means that both mother and baby have the opportunity to ease into the new routine. Some jobs are ideal for job-sharing, which means that two mothers can reap the benefits of part-time work.

Sometimes you'll find that your profit margin when you get back to work is not great — by the time you have paid for childcare, travel, clothing, convenience foods and possibly cleaning — and you'll wonder what on earth you are doing. You might find yourself thinking about other alternatives such as working from home, but if you are considering this kind of change, give it careful thought. You already have a lot on your plate and now may not be the time to start adapting to new work routines. Although you might find it an easy transition, it won't do any harm to think it through properly and weigh up the pros and cons.

Working from home

Some women like to work from home when a child is small while others need to be in quite a separate space to get on with the job, particularly with a baby who can be both distracting and demanding. There are distinct advantages and disadvantages and also some difficulties to overcome.

Although you might feel as though your life is ruled by the clock when you have to go out to your work, often you'll find it easier with a small child to have definite and regular working hours. Working from home,

When you're a mother who works from home

Advantages	Disadvantages
•You can keep your child at home with you rather than sending her to childcare.	•You might find it difficult to work with a baby around.
•You can be on hand in case of sickness.	•It's hard not to feel divided if your work is staring you in the face.
•You can keep the household and housework more under control.	•When faced with a job you don't want to do, you can end up eith a sparkling clean house at the end of the day and no paid work done.
•You can keep your own hours.	•Your own hours can be very long.

particularly in jobs where there are deadlines involved, can mean that your working life can very easily start to take over your family time. You can't afford to say 'no', you can't afford to stop and it's extremely difficult to find a balance to the conflicting demands of home and work.

'I find that for months at a time I work every day of the week and I don't think it's good for either my family or for me. I try and kid myself that my hours are more flexible working this way and I suppose in some senses they are — I can get to school by 3.30 p.m. most days but then I work well into the night. I feel that the pressure never stops.'

In the workplace

Although it may not seem so at first, what being a working mother almost inevitably does for you is help you to make better use of your time simply because there is so little of it. You'll find you have to be more organised and learn to prioritise in order to get it all done.

You can't assume that everyone will understand your situation and you might need to make it clear that you can't work back because of family commitments or that you can't take work home with you. It can be difficult for you when you feel under pressure, particularly when it's because of the workload rather than the people. In places that are understaffed or are working to deadline it's hard to walk out and leave everyone else to it but, in most cases, you'll find your colleagues understanding. When they're not you'll simply have to tough it out and remind yourself what your priorities are.

'What I notice about working mothers when they're at work is that they don't waste any time sharpening their pencils. They get right down to it and also seem to have the ability to deal with any problems that arise fairly painlessly and practically.'

ATTITUDES AT WORK

There are so many working mothers these days that their presence in the workplace is no longer an issue. Most of us don't have to worry about what to do with a boss who thinks a mother should be at home with her children or the one who thinks you should be working 60 hours a week. If you do find yourself in such a situation, the only realistic thing to do is start looking for another job where you can comfortably be who you are.

'I went for an interview as a speech writer and the general manager asked me to tell him about my work ethic. I didn't really know what he meant. I replied that I was willing to put in overtime and to take work home with me but not to compromise my family life. When I phoned to find out if I got the job, he said that although I have excellent qualifications, my other commitments presented a problem.'

Many workplaces have changed and softened, too, because more mothers have taken on management roles and more men have become involved in their own family life. While it hasn't happened everywhere, we can look to it as an encouraging and concrete result of our combined efforts as parents to integrate our home and working lives.

'As a mother and a manager I find that I now have a more personal and family approach at work. It feels less officious and more congenial — but I don't think it's more organised.'

Working out of work

While this may not be a problem for a lot of women, some of you may find that your work can take over, particularly if you are in a position where you can take on extra work to earn extra money. Your evenings and weekends can be easily eaten up either making up for what you feel you should have done during a working day or because you think you will benefit from a casual pay packet as well. The result, of course, is that there's no time to unwind and no time for leisure.

In addition to the problem of time, you will also feel more stressed, particularly if you're working to a deadline. Often, too, it's self-defeating financially because you end up paying more to compensate for your loss of time and energy, for example buying takeaway food more often. When you're offered extra work, think carefully about whether you and your family will come out ahead.

'I am weak when it comes to saying "no" to working longer hours and I short-change my son when it comes to time in order to carry out work duties. The reverse never applies because he is minded by a nanny I like and trust. It's sad but I seem to need the approval of the people at work more than I need his.'

Is work taking over your life?

Try this quick quiz to see whether you are in control of your working life.

Give yourself one point for each 'yes'.

1 Have you done the grocery shopping after 6 p.m. more than once this month?

2 Do you feel bad that you owe phone calls to more than three people?

3 Have all your pot plants died?

4 Do you find yourself wishing for a brief illness so you could spend a few days in bed?

5 Do you get anxious when it's time to get the car serviced?

6 Do all the takeaway food places in your neighbourhood know you by name?

7 Have you put off making a dentist's appointment because there's no time?

8 If given the choice of working fewer hours for the same money or more hours for more money, would you take the money?

9 Have you taken work home with you more than twice in the last month?

10 Have you ever found yourself thinking about work during sex?

HOW DID YOU SCORE?

10 points:	It's time to look hard at work and the balance in your life.
7 to 9 points:	Things could be worse, but not much.
4 to 6 points:	Room to improve.
3 points or less:	You're doing okay. Keep it up.

When your child is sick

Probably one of the most stressful things for you as a working mother is anticipating the possibility of your child getting sick. Then all the dilemmas and guilt can come crashing down on you as you're torn most dreadfully between your work and family commitments.

Some employers will allow you to use your own sick leave to care for your sick child. Others will permit some flexibility and you will be able to take work home with you or to make the time up. If you are able to take it in turns with your partner and your children are basically healthy, you should be able to manage using your own leave. You'll find that generally few working days are lost unless, of course, your child is very sick or sick for a long period of time.

Sometimes work schedules don't allow for the flexibility of taking a day off and sometimes bosses aren't too understanding. A sick child doesn't usually give you much warning and often it's a case of discovering at 7 a.m. that you've got a problem on your hands.

If you set up your backstops beforehand you will eliminate an extra stress. Your first choice may well not be available on the day, so have a few possibilities lined up. You might make arrangements for emergencies with grandparents. You could establish a regular babysitter who might be available to come to the house during the day as well as at night. You might wish to investigate the babysitting services which you'll find in the Yellow Pages. Give a few a call and ask some basic questions about rates, how much notice they need and the credentials of the carers so that you'll know where you stand should a real emergency arise. The last thing you'll want to do when you have a sick child and a pressing deadline at work is to have to start hunting for someone who's prepared to look after a sick child.

You'll probably find that your child will always manage to get sick the week you start a new job or the day when you are absolutely indispensable at work. Think through well beforehand how you will deal with these predicaments depending on what is wrong with her and how sick she is.

Obviously there will be times when she's really ill and needs the security of one of her parents caring for her. Other times being with familiar and loving grandparents or your regular babysitter will be fine.

LEAVING HER AT HOME ALONE

The age at which you'll feel you can safely leave your child at home alone will vary, depending on you, your situation and the child herself. But when you do, be sure to consider the arrangements.

- Make sure there's a phone close by the bed or sofa where she's lying.

- Tell her you'll phone during the day and do so.

- Make sure she has your and your partner's phone numbers in case of an emergency. Leave another backup number like a neighbour's or grandparent's in case you can't be contacted.

- Ask a neighbour or relative to look in during the day to make sure everything is all right.

- Leave some food already prepared, like some sandwiches and some fruit.

- Make sure there's entertainment to keep her subdued, like some videos, comics or magazines.

- Make sure that she will be either warm enough or cool enough during the day.

NOT SO SICK

You'll find there'll be those borderline cases when you feel sure that if it wasn't for work, you'd let her stay at home and just have some general R and R. You know with yourself that sometimes taking a day to revive can prevent you getting sick.

Vague symptoms are often the order of the day and when you're rushing to get to work you don't have much time to deliberate. When you are in any real doubt, take the day off. Otherwise you will spend your day feeling wretched and you certainly won't be focused on work.

There'll be times too when she just plain doesn't want to go to school and sickness seems the best way out. There's no easy way of telling when she's putting it on, although you do get more practised over time. Some medical services open early for quick consultations without appointments and a visit there on the way could mean you are just late for work instead of having to take a whole day off. Also, you can always rely on the school to let you know if she is ill during the day and can't soldier on but you do run the risk of seeming callous. Thankfully anyone who knows anything about children realises that their health can change within minutes and that diagnosing a child's symptoms can sometimes even be beyond a doctor.

'It was four years ago now but I still feel bad about it. My son kept complaining that he felt sick and I thought he was up to his old tricks, so I sent him to school saying that I felt sure they'd call if he needed to come home. I no sooner got to work than someone at the school phoned to say he had vomited all over the child in front of him in morning assembly.'

When there is a crisis

Some women think it's better to keep quiet when all hell breaks loose at home because they think it reflects badly on them as workers if their mother role is falling apart. Honesty is undoubtedly the best policy when it comes to personal problems, though, if it is likely that they will affect your work in some way. Also simply because something happens to you doesn't mean you aren't in control — being in control is how you go about dealing with it.

If you have a crisis because your childminder has eloped, it's going to have some bearing on your working hours as well as your emotional state and you are more than likely going to be distracted until you have sorted things out. If you have a child who has just come down with chickenpox, everyone will understand that you need some time to organise emergency childcare.

When your child is very ill, things become clear-cut for you in terms of taking time off work. It's obvious where your priorities will lie when things are critical but it will again become a dilemma once she starts to recuperate. If it's a lengthy period, you might feel that you are wearing out the goodwill of family and friends. If paid help is too expensive an option, you or your partner may have to look at restructuring your or his working life.

'My son had to have an operation, and I took the week off that he was in hospital and my husband took the week off that he got home. Then my mother was able to come and look after him for the last week before he went back to school.'

CHAPTER 9

WHEN YOU'RE PREGNANT

Not only are the streets suddenly filled with mothers and babies and the escalators oozing strollers but everyone at work turns out to be either a parent or very, very clucky. With all the laying on of hands and well-wishing, this child of yours will most certainly be blessed.

Work-related health

If you are fit and well then there's no good reason not to work during your pregnancy. The only reasons to stop are to do with your health and the health of the baby, so if you have had previous experiences of miscarriage or birth complications, you will want to check with your doctor to find out what she or he advises.

Of course, some jobs do have health risks attached and with these you'll need to consider whether to seek a transfer or some alternative employment for the duration of your pregnancy. If you are already working in one of these areas, it's likely that you will already be aware of the health risks but the jobs that you'll want to think carefully about include:

- strenuous ones, such as being a nurse in a ward where you have to lift heavy patients;

- those where you come into contact with potentially toxic chemicals or materials, such as lead, mercury or anaesthetic gases;

- those where you come into contact with high levels of radiation, such as being a health worker dealing with X-rays or being an airport baggage-scanner attendant;

- those where you can come into contact with potentially harmful infections, such as being a worker in a laboratory;

- those demanding excessively long shifts where you don't get the opportunity to sit down, such as being a waitress.

Some women are concerned about working with photocopiers and VDUs during pregnancy because of the low levels of radiation emitted from them. You can take extra care by making sure you always have the lid firmly closed when you are photocopying so you aren't exposed to the light, and either limiting your work at a computer terminal if you can or seeing if you can have a more protective screen fitted.

Travelling to work

You may find that you have to make a change in how you get to and from work when you are in the later stages of your pregnancy. Riding on a busy bus or train might not be particularly comfortable when you are large.

You need to recognise now that later on you may have to find alternatives to buses and trains, such as driving yourself to work or catching the occasional taxi.

Also be prepared for the fact that the days of chivalry are gone and that if you are thinking someone in a bus or train will get up to give you their seat because you are quite obviously pregnant, you could be waiting a long time. More often than not you'll find you are forced to ask politely for someone to relinquish their perch, explaining that you are pregnant in case they haven't noticed.

> 'The only bad part about being pregnant and working was travelling to and from work — particularly towards the end. I found the train trips very tiring, particularly at peak hour, and I was bustled and jostled and no one but no one would give me their seat.'

When to tell

There is a lot to be said for not telling people at work for quite some time that you are pregnant. Apart from anything else, you will find that your pregnancy can seem interminable, and while you will be filled with your exciting news at the start, after seven or eight months you will be sick and tired of being asked 'How much longer?'

On the other hand, giving your employers notice of your pregnancy allows them the chance to organise what arrangements they will make for your maternity leave. Of course, if you suffer from morning sickness and it affects your working hours, or you have to change some of your duties, then you will have to let your employers know fairly promptly.

> 'I suppose I didn't really think about it before so I was surprised at how supportive and celebratory people were at my work when I told them I was pregnant. It's funny how it brings out the softest side of even the ones that seem so tough.'

When to stop

Most women need to keep working for as long as possible for financial reasons and while you remain healthy there is no good reason to change your lifestyle at this stage. To qualify for maternity pay you'll need to work up until a certain time before the baby is due. Maternity leave awards vary, so you'll need to make sure that you find out from your personnel department what the requirements are for you to qualify and what your and their responsibilities are.

Don't be surprised if you wake up one day and feel that you can't drag your huge body around much longer and that the last thing you want to do is go to work. You just long to lie on the sofa all day.

Physical changes

In the first three months it's quite likely you'll feel overwhelmed by tiredness. Think of this as preparation for how you'll feel after the baby is born. Some women also suffer from a feeling of nausea or morning sickness — although it can happen at any time during the day. Try increasing your intake of B-vitamin foods. Follow your cravings but not to excess and eat little but often.

Emotional changes

Some women tend to feel more emotional when they're pregnant. It's not always noticeable to other people and unlikely to have any effect on your job but it's reassuring to know that it's par for the course and that you aren't going crazy.

Tackling tiredness

Your pregnancy is a good time to start the practice of looking after yourself. Pay attention to what your body is telling you — slow down and take it easy. Follow these tips on not getting too tired.

- It might sound drastic but it helps if you cut back on your social life.

- Sleep — go to bed early and have naps on weekends.

- Rest as much as possible during the day and lie on the floor at lunchtime if you can or put your feet up on a stool. Practise your relaxation exercises.

- Force yourself to take tea-breaks, even if you are desperately busy.

- To unwind, lie down on the sofa for half an hour as soon as you get home or soak in a bath.

- Ask for help around the home — from your children, your partner, family and friends. Involve them in the cooking, washing, shopping and cleaning.

- If you work at a desk, make sure you have proper support for your back and your feet and move around during the day to stretch your legs.

- If your work involves a lot of standing or sitting, put your feet up or lie down when you get an opportunity.

Keeping fit

Now is not the time to give up on your regular exercise program, and if you aren't doing any, it's a good time to look out for antenatal exercise or yoga classes. You'll find they'll stand you in very good stead when it comes to the birth and it will also get you into the habit of taking the time to keep your body strong and healthy that you'll need as a working mother.

Also take opportunities at work to exercise when you can. Take the stairs instead of the lift, walk with a friend in the fresh air at lunchtime and move about and stretch when you can.

Antenatal care and classes

Although these are important for all mothers, whether working or not, the difference is that you will have to schedule them into your working life. Check-ups and classes can pose problems for you if your work is a long way from home and your hospital. Check-ups can be time-consuming and you'll find that the doctor is often running late. Schedule appointments early or late if possible and let them know at work where you will be going in case there are any delays.

An antenatal class is a good place to start building a network of other parents if this is your first child. Having other parents with babies the same age can be considerable support early on — to call on, to share childcare and information, and to share experiences. (Later you'll meet other working parents through childcare, preschools and schools.)

Maternity leave

Even if you aren't absolutely sure whether you'll be going back to work after the baby is born, it's best to keep your options open. It's generally much easier to have a job to return to and people that you're familiar with when you have a small child.

Maternity leave awards vary in the amounts of paid and unpaid leave and also with regard to returning to work part-time. Make sure you investigate all your leave options through either your personnel department or union rep and consider asking for leave without pay if you want a longer period.

You may want to take as long a maternity leave as you feel you can afford financially, or you may be one of those women who miss the pulse of the workplace. Be prepared to be flexible because it's not always easy to predict which way you'll fall until you find yourself in the situation. Sometimes those most determined not to miss a beat when they have a baby find that their feelings change dramatically once he's arrived and others find that they are itching to get back to work (and hot cups of coffee) well before their maternity leave is over.

'I work as a freelancer and there's no such thing as maternity leave for me. I work in an industry where it's out of sight out of mind, so I was back at work part-time ten weeks after my baby was born. I even found myself breastfeeding in a budget meeting. Luckily I was surrounded by supportive and interested people.'

Plan with your partner

It may well seem premature but now is the time to start planning with your partner how you are going to share childcare and household responsibilities when your baby is born. Don't for a minute imagine that things will stay the same when you have another person to care for. You'll find it difficult enough then to adjust to your new way of life without having to negotiate what your new roles will be.

Remember, too, that after you have spent some time at home with your baby it's quite likely that you will have taken on some more of the domestic duties simply because you are there. You'll need to consider and talk about how this will change for both you and your partner when you return to work. It sounds ridiculously simple but the fairest way is to make a list and work out who will do what so that there's no cause for conflict.

CHAPTER 10

THE CHILDCARE YEARS

Ask any working mother — peace of mind comes with good childcare arrangements but finding what you want, where and when you need it is like finding the proverbial needle in a haystack. Now, suddenly, you can understand why you always see the mothers and fathers of young children standing in the corner of the kitchen at parties swapping childcare stories instead of jokes.

The search for childcare

As crazy as it sounds, it's a good idea to start investigating your childcare options well in advance of your return to work. If you are returning soon after your baby is born, you should start looking and booking while you are still pregnant, particularly if you are interested in centre-based or family day-care services as they generally have very long waiting lists (of up to three years).

Once upon a time the cost of private home-based care or nannies was too high for most people to consider but, now, because of relatively high childcare centre fees, it has become a reasonable option for some. Of course, this doesn't require quite as much forethought, although you will need to have worked out well in advance that this is the way you definitely want to and can afford to go. You may find that other avenues are already closed by the time you've changed your mind. Frequently mothers rely on friends and family to look after their children while they work because lack of availability of other kinds of care or their cost makes it their only option.

If you are wanting to use a childcare centre or family day-care scheme, make sure you put your name on a number of lists because you may not get into your first choice. Once on a list for a centre that you are keen to get into keep calling them and keep in touch. This is one of those situations where persistence generally pays off. Unfortunately though, when the time comes, you may find that you aren't left with a lot of choice when it comes to location or even choosing a centre that you feel suits you and you like.

While childcare centres take applications all year round you have a better chance of starting your child off at the beginning of a year when the top age range of children move on to school. This means movement in the other age ranges and, therefore, vacancies. You might consider placing your child in part-time care before your planned return to work, in a centre where you want to take up a full-time place. This will give you a better chance of getting full-time care there when you need it.

You'll probably have to accept the fact that finding the childcare is going to be your responsibility because few men seem to grasp the urgency of the childcare issue at this early stage. The task of investigating the options, checking them out and finally making a decision most often falls to mother. Even if you're determined that your partner makes some moves and you hold off, you may find it's to no avail because when the crunch comes, you are the one who needs to go back to work and you are the one sweating on the care.

The pain of leaving

No matter how much you might be looking forward to getting back to work and no matter how much you might believe in the benefits of childcare, leaving your baby is going to be hard at first. You mightn't think so but it'll be hard, too, when she starts school, high school and leaves home but now her size and vulnerability will make it doubly difficult. Your feelings, too, will be intensified depending on how satisfied you are with the childcare you have found and how much you enjoy your job.

 'I have to keep reminding myself that my mum worked and I turned out okay.'

You will be relieved to know that there's no ideal age to start your baby in childcare. As your return to work is most often dictated by either your work itself or your financial situation, there's no need to add to your worries by thinking that you've done it at the wrong time. As with so many of these things, there's no right or wrong but what is important is how you feel about it and how you approach it.

Arrange for any type of care to start about a week before you go back to work so that both you and your baby have a chance to settle into your new routines. If the baby is being minded in your home, this will mean that you can overlap with the carer and it will give you a chance to show her the ropes.

There are of course going to be times when your baby is going to be unhappy when you leave her but this will happen whether you are working or not. You'll find that at the age of eight months, for example, babies often suffer what is known as 'separation anxiety' and they like to keep mother constantly within their sight.

Remember that if your baby isn't used to being left by you with friends, family or babysitter before she starts at childcare, then she has a lot to cope with at once. It's better to give her the opportunity to spend time in the care of other adults from an early age. Taking her to play group while you are on maternity leave will also give her the opportunity to interact with groups of children.

There will inevitably be times when she is quite distressed when you leave and this can last from anything from a few days to a few weeks. This is a hideous phase for both of you — as well as for the carer. The reassuring thing, as carers will tell you, is that her crying and misery usually stop once you are out of sight, and although you may well spend the rest of the day feeling wretched, she'll quite happily move on to other things (and people).

Always be honest and straightforward about what you are doing by saying goodbye directly to her and telling her you're off to work now. It's important that, right from the start, she learns to trust her childcare arrangements and that she understands that she is there while you go to work and that you will come every day to pick her up. Don't slip out hoping she won't notice or be upset. As distressing as it might be it's better that she sees you go, has a good cry, and then gets on with her day instead of wondering what has happened.

As well as the pain …

As well as the inevitable pain you will feel at leaving your baby you will almost certainly experience feelings of guilt and anxiety — even when you think you are quite comfortable with the notion of going back to work and having someone else look after your child. We have grown up in our society with strong sentiments about mothers being the sole carers of their children until they are about three years old and it's almost impossible for these not to have some effect on us.

Some mothers are also concerned that the childminder will take on a significant role in their baby's life and that they will be 'replaced', particularly if it's one-to-one care. Remind yourself that the bond you have with your baby won't be changed and that it's only a question of another loving adult entering her life.

'You realise early on that it's ridiculous for you to feel jealous of a carer. If your child is happy and has a good and happy relationship with her, then there's no reason for you not to be happy. Imagine how it would feel if they didn't like each other. And, after all, you are still "mum".'

'He sees her as someone who cares for him and it doesn't bother me that he has formed an attachment to her. There is no confusion for him and our bond is strong enough to withstand other attachments.'

Your choices

Childcare for working parents of preschool children covers a wide range of situations, both informal and formal. You might opt for your partner, grandparents, a friend, a nanny, a childcare centre or family day care. Then, later, when they are older there are kindergartens and preschools to consider.

'For any type of childcare to work well you have to be able to communicate easily with the carer or carers.'

The basic difference between informal and formal services is that informal arrangements are usually provided in either the child's or the carer's home. They are based on a personal agreement, often with friends or family but also with nannies. Formal services operate outside the child's home in either a centre or family day-care service and they have to meet State and local government licensing regulations.

A major consideration when it comes to making your choice is the hours of operation — many centres don't suit a lot of working parents because their hours are 8.30 a.m. to 5.30 p.m., which doesn't leave much of a margin for travelling time. Some have extended hours of operation, and family day care can often be more flexible, as are private arrangements with family, friends or nannies.

You'll find, too, that your child's and your needs may change over time and you'll have to look at other possibilities. Some mothers, for example, like to start their babies off in the more intimate atmosphere of family day care or staying with a relative but then find the time comes (at about two) when their child is ready to move on to the larger social environment of a centre. If they have spent their early years in childcare, they may become bored with their centre at about three years of age and be ready to move on to the 'outside' world and you may have to consider a move to yet another centre.

'The benefits of childcare for me are the freedoms it allows me and the peace of mind it gives me. For my son they are that he is learning socialisation and how to interact with others. The disadvantage is that my son isn't spending his days with me, his mother.'

Whatever your childcare arrangements, the basics that you would expect to be provided for your child are:

• proper physical care like food and drink;

• body and clothes kept reasonably (but not fastidiously) clean;

• some exercise and naps;

• intellectual stimulation and play;

• involvement and interaction with the carer/s;

• some degree of affection and warmth.

Childcare centres

Day care, long day care, nurseries, creches — childcare centres go by a variety of names, each offering a variety of services. Across the board they provide care for babies from six weeks old to school age but not all centres take babies — some start at one year old and others at three.

Some people prefer the idea of babies being in a one-to-one situation because they get more attention. If you have ever seen the loving attention that babies get in childcare centres, from both staff and older children, you would quickly change your mind if you had thought they were being disadvantaged.

Centres are generally open five days a week but they close on public holidays and for a couple of weeks over Christmas. They offer full-time care but some also have a number of part-time places and irregular or occasional care. Opening hours vary, with a few even operating 24 hours a day for shift workers. They can be government-funded, employer-sponsored or privately run. Government-funded centres have a list of priorities that they must follow when giving places in the centre and this includes both parents working.

In order to get government registration, centres have to comply with regulations covering things like the premises and staffing. Staff ratios vary from State to State but most childcare centres operate on a ratio of 5:1 for children under two, 8:1 for two- to three-year-olds, and 10:1 for three- to five-year-olds. One advantage in it not being a one-to-one situation is that there is less likelihood of a personality clash between carer and child which, in an extreme case, could result in you having to change your childcare arrangements. Obviously, too, there is always backup when staff members are sick which means you aren't left in the lurch.

In government-funded centres, most of the staff have or are getting formal qualifications and they are kept up to date with in-service training. You can feel sure that the programs they develop for the children will be educationally stimulating and age-appropriate. Many centres now have male staff which provides a welcome balance in the care and nurturing of small children.

Costs for centres vary according to what it costs to run that particular centre and service but the average cost for full day care (without any government fee relief) is around $140 a week. (Please note: this figure may change; this figure and the others in this chapter were accurate at the time of writing in December 1994.)

There are an increasing number of employers who are either establishing their own centres or buying places in established ones for their women workers. Some cater for shifts and rosters and have either 24-hour or extended-hour care which generally operates from 6 a.m. to 10 p.m.

The advantages of work-based centres are the proximity of parent to child, for visits (and breastfeeding) and in the case of emergencies; that the children can spend more time with their parents, although this is usually travelling time; and that the hours of the centre are suited to the workplace. The advantages of community-based centres are that you can change jobs more easily and your children can develop contacts with the whole of the local community.

FEE RELIEF

Childcare assistance or fee relief is available through the Commonwealth government for families on low and middle incomes. Services need to be 'approved' and can be childcare centres, family day care, or out-of-school care. Obviously, you can assume that government-funded centres will have met the necessary criteria, but you will need to check whether privately run centres have been approved.

The level of assistance will depend on your family income, the number of dependent children you have, the number of children you have in approved family day-care schemes or childcare centres, and the hours of care you need. If the centre charges a higher hourly fee than the level set by the government, then the parents have to pay the difference or gap. The childcare service bills the government directly for their share and you pay your share directly to the service. The childcare service will be able to help you with applications and information or you can contact the Department of Social Security, which you will find listed in the White Pages.

In addition, parents can claim the Childcare Cash Rebate for work-related childcare costs of up to $28.20 for one child and $61.20 for two or more each week. This is administered by the Health Insurance Commission and parents register with Medicare.

Family day care

Family day care allows for children to be looked after in the homes of registered carers. The scheme is licensed and funded by the government and usually operates through local councils, State governments or voluntary organisations. A carer can have a maximum of five children, including her own, but this can vary from state to state. She is given support and backup by the scheme's administrators who visit her regularly. If you have any doubts or questions you feel you can't ask your carer, it is probably best to go to the scheme coordinator.

The administrators of the scheme are the ones responsible for matching carers and families. They will generally give you a couple of names to follow up of carers who suit your needs. The cost of family day care varies but the average is about $100 a week (40 hours) and, as with government-funded centres, families who are eligible can apply for fee relief under the Commonwealth Childcare Assistance Scheme if they are in approved schemes and they can also claim the Childcare Cash Rebate for work-related childcare costs.

'Because I'm a single mother, I liked the idea of my son going to family day care and being in more of a 'family' situation. I felt it was as close to being at home as he could get — with a backyard and grass and flowers, trips to the corner store and one main carer (apart from me).'

What to look for

You will be more productive at work when you know your child is safe and secure. Here's a list of things to consider to help you when you are looking for care.

- Visit at different times of the day, for example at mealtimes, mid-morning, or late afternoon when children are likely to be tired so you can see how the carer handles these situations.

- Do the children look happy?

- Are the toys and premises safe?

- Is it a smoke-free environment?

- Is the food nutritious?

- How are the children disciplined?

- Are any problems openly discussed with parents?

- What will happen when the carer or child is sick?

- Have you any recommendations or references for the carer?

- What's the play area like — indoors and outdoors?

- What are the rest or sleep areas like?

- Is there a television and is it often on?

Nannies

Employing a nanny to look after your child or children in your own home is becoming a more popular option for many working parents. It not only allows more flexibility and gives your child the security of being in her own home, in a one-to-one or one-to-two situation, but it has also become a more attractive financial proposition with increases in childcare centre fees. Some parents choose to share a nanny with another couple, with the nanny looking after the children in one or other of their homes.

Having someone either living in or spending long hours in your house every day can be a tall order, though, and there are some things you'll need to consider.

- You should be able to sit down together and discuss the children and things like discipline and bedtimes.

- The employer/employee role should be clearly defined and not forgotten. Remember, you are still the employer when you're wearing your nightgown.

- While a nanny may well become a part of the family, there are also times she'll need to understand when to make herself scarce — like when you and your partner are having one of your 'animated discussions'.

- Just because she is there, you shouldn't take advantage of her — make sure she has her time off, let her know what you are doing and when you are running late. While one of the joys of having a nanny is your not being so conscious of time, you should show consideration for her and recognise when her working day ends.

- You'll have to learn to put up with her annoying personal habits just as she'll have to put up with yours.

- Be aware of her employment situation and think about whether it's fair, and whether the set-up suits her and gives her job satisfaction.

FINDING A NANNY

You can find a nanny via an agency, you can advertise in the newspaper or answer an ad, or contact a nanny school or TAFE college that trains childcare workers. You can have either live-in, live-out or part-time nannies.

Make sure you discuss payment first off because you don't want to go through the exercise of the interview and find the perfect nanny only to discover that you can't afford her or, indeed, that you can't afford anyone. There is no minimum wage for nannies and payment varies enormously depending on qualifications and experience. A live-in nanny employed via an agency can cost between $250 and $400 for a five-day week; a part-time and live-out nanny can cost from $7 to $14 an hour or from $400 to $600 a week.

If you use an agency they will vet the candidates for you and send ones that they think are suitable. Generally, an agency's placement fee is about the same as the nanny's gross weekly wage.

If you advertise, expect a fairly large response (between 40 and 50) that you will have to weed your way through. Have a list of basic questions that you can ask in the initial phone call so you can cull quickly. You will have specific questions to suit your particular situation but these are some you may want to ask.

- What training, if any, have you had?

- What experience do you have?

- Do you have a driver's licence?

- Do you have references?

- Do you smoke?

Interview the prospective nanny at least once and don't be timid about following up references. It's vital that you feel you have all the information you need and that you've made the right decision. If you like you can ask for a trial period, say six weeks, to make sure that this is what you both want. In this case you could pay the nanny her casual rate, and if you hired her through an agency, you would also need to pay the daily service fee (which may be refundable if you decide to take her on permanently).

DECIDING WHAT YOU WANT

To help you work out what matters most to you in a nanny, make a list of the qualities you have in mind. Would you prefer someone that's older and more grandmotherly or someone young? Does it matter to you how old they are? Would you prefer someone who has brought up her own children?

Beforehand, think about how you are going to find out in an interview what you need to know. Remember, though, that what's most important is to watch how the prospective nanny relates to your little darling. While an initial meeting won't tell all, it will give some indication of the nanny's feelings about children, and for that matter how your child feels about her. If you are interviewing for a live-in nanny, it is essential that your partner meets them before you both finally make up your minds. After all, he will be living with her too.

Some things to ask in the interview (if they haven't already been covered on the phone) are as follows.

- What are your qualifications?

- What experience have you had?

- Are you comfortable about driving with a young child in the car?

- How do you think children should be disciplined?

- What would you do in a typical day?

- Are you prepared to do light housework, like tidying and doing the washing-up?

- How long would you plan to work for me as a nanny?

'The questions I asked at the interview were almost irrelevant because I was much more interested in seeing how she interacted with my son. What I wanted to find out was whether she was someone who had an obvious and honest interest in children because I wanted to think that she would be involved with and develop a genuine affection for him.'

Employing a nanny

Now that you're an employer there are several things you need to be aware of.

• Live-in nannies have at least one and a half days off a week and, generally, two.

• They are entitled to four weeks' paid annual leave and five days' paid sick leave.

• Standard rates apply for one or two children but you should expect to pay more for three or more children.

• If you're paying an employee more than $100 a week you are legally required to register as a group employer and withhold tax — the Australian Tax Office will give you all the information you need.

• While may nannies prefer cash in hand, if you do pay tax on her earnings and she has a tax file number, she can register with Medicare as a carer and you can claim the Childcare Cash Rebate.

• You may be required to pay 4 per cent superannuation. Ask either the agency or the Tax Office about requirements.

• You should be covered for domestic workers' compensation and have public liability cover — either through your household policy, the agency or a separate policy.

• Her personal belongings won't be covered by your home contents insurance policy because she isn't 'family' so find out what additional arrangements you need to make.

• If she will be driving your car, make sure your insurance covers her. If she is under 25, you will probably have to pay an additional premium.

• You'll need to make sure she always has a cash float for outings and emergencies.

• Don't expect that she'll save you the cost of having a cleaner. While you may be able to make arrangements with her to keep the home tidy, do some shopping and perhaps even keep the laundry under control, major cleaning is out. Remind yourself that her job is to look after your child, not clean the house.

'I had a live-in nanny for the first 18 months after I went back to work. I felt that it offered my son continuity and stability and it also made it much easier for me. My job is pretty demanding and it helped that I could walk straight out the door in the mornings and not have to worry too much in the evenings if I was 15 minutes or so late.'

Your partner

It is becoming increasingly common for men to stay at home and care for their small children. Sometimes it's because they have more flexible working situations and sometimes because they find themselves out of the workforce altogether.

For whatever reason, the overwhelming response seems to be that they enjoy the opportunity to spend this time with their family. For your part, though, it's now too late to think about the selection process for the childcare and you can't be too picky about how they go about it. You will just have to come to terms with the fact that it's them and not you.

'I sometimes wonder if I'm just one of those people who'll never be happy. We decided long beforehand that my partner would stay at home with our baby and I would be the one to go out to work because he can more easily do his work from home. He's happy, the baby's happy but now I feel as though I am the one missing out.'

Private home-based care

In addition to having a nanny or your partner providing the care, there are other possibilities for home-based private care. Most of these involve relatives or friends and you will need to think about the advantages and disadvantages as carefully as you would when choosing any other form of childcare.

For many parents, this is the cheapest and, sometimes, only available option. If it's not your first choice of care but you can't afford anything else (or are unable to get a place for your child in a childcare centre or family day care), you will probably find that you have some hurdles to negotiate — or to bypass and learn to live with. You may find it difficult to establish the kind of care you want for your child. Grandparents can be particularly touchy on this subject and can have firm ideas on how to bring up children properly — after all they've already done a fabulous job with you or their son. You may hit a bit of emotional blackmail and find that you are supposed to feel obligated and eternally grateful for what they are doing for you.

Even if it is your first choice, you're still going to have to work some things out. It's very important that you feel comfortable about the way the person will be raising your child. For this kind of care to work out well, you'll have to reach a basic agreement about how children should be brought up and you'll need to be confident that if you do have a problem, you will be able to talk about it and that your suggestions will be taken in good spirit and not as criticisms.

It's also important, however, that you give the minders some freedom to look after the child in their own way. Of course you should make your expectations clear — such as routines for sleeping and feeding, what kind of activities you'd like them to do and so on — but they shouldn't feel that you are writing their scripts and directing their every move. You'll need to trust them to do a good job and let them know that you have confidence in them.

A main disadvantage in any such private arrangements is that you are stuck if the carer gets sick. You'll need to have some backup arrangement.

The main advantages of this kind of arrangement for your child are that she can enjoy the familiarity and comforts of home; that she can attend local playgroups; that she can get to know the neighbourhood, local shops and parks; and, on this one-to-one basis, she'll get lots of attention. If you have a choice, make sure that the carer will be able to provide these advantages.

Some advantages for you are:

- having more flexibility in your hours and not having to worry so much about being on time at the end of the day;

- not having to take time off work when your child is too sick to be taken out;

- less chance of your child picking up all those colds and infections that children encounter in their first months of contact with other small children at childcare;

- having more say in how you want things done and what routine you would like followed;

- possibly having help with household chores like sterilising bottles, putting on a load of washing or doing the shopping.

YOUR HOUSE OR THEIRS?

If your child is going to be minded at someone else's house, you will need to make sure that the premises are safe for your child. People who aren't used to having young children around can easily forget that babies will put the most unlikely things in their mouths and could stick almost anything into an unused power point. You may need to supply your carer with some safety devices such as childproof cupboard locks or safety plugs for power points. You can get information about child safety from the Child Accident Prevention Foundation of Australia.

As well as safety, you may want to look at:

- where your child will be having her sleeps;

- her play space — both indoors and outdoors;

- whether or not you will have to bring her toys with you;

- whether there are any pets and how they behave with children.

How to approach problems

The care of your child is one of the most sensitive issues you are ever likely to face and it's very easy to be very emotional about it. If you aren't happy with some aspect of your child's care, approach the subject carefully. Of course your concerns are important but bear in mind that the carer may well be trying to do what she thinks is best and will be hurt if she thinks you are being critical.

It's possible to phrase problems in a way that isn't too high-handed and doesn't undermine her. Instead of 'Don't do that' and 'Do this', try:

- 'I've found that she really likes...'

- 'I've found that this works well...'

- 'I think she's eating too many sweet things so would you mind...'

- 'I think she's old enough now to...'

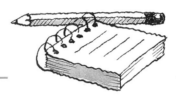

Babysitting

You are going to need the occasional care of a babysitter, as well as your regular childcare arrangements during working hours. It's important that you have regular leisure time away from your child. If you have a partner it's vital that you spend time alone together away from the demands of home and if you are single you need some space as well.

Babysitters can be found by word of mouth, through local papers and, often, local agencies. You might have friends with teenage children eager to earn some cash. You might like to think about setting up a babysitting co-op that works on a barter system and saves you money. You earn credits for babysitting someone else's children and points are debited when someone babysits yours.

Basic commonsense prevails when hiring a babysitter — like letting them know where you'll be, leaving emergency contact numbers, making sure they will be warm and well fed and watered, and returning home when you said you would.

CHAPTER 11

BREASTFEEDING AND WORK

You love the way your baby suckles at your breast and stares into your eyes like there's no one else in the world. From those soft warm feelings you have to move to the harsh reality of cold, hard breast pumps and lugging your daily produce home in a cold storage pack. It's hardly the romantic vision of breastfeeding you'd imagined.

Returning to work

Your return to work may well come before you are ready to wean your baby, and although some will have it that working and breastfeeding are incompatible, that's not necessarily the case. If your milk supply is well established it's unlikely that it will dry up when you stop demand feeding. Another reason given for working and breastfeeding not being a good idea is that it makes you tired. This one doesn't seem to make much sense as it's pretty hard to avoid being tired when you are a new working mother.

> 'One of the things that worried me most in thinking about when I would go back to work was having to wean my baby early. The conventional wisdom was that it would be too hard to keep breastfeeding — that I would be exhausted and that my milk would dry up. It turned out to be very easy.'

Don't be put off from the start by the thought of it all being too difficult because many women don't find it a problem at all. Planning your return to work and how you will continue breastfeeding is what will make the difference. Getting the hang of it may involve a little trial and error but take the time to work out what suits both you and your baby best and seek advice from a Nursing Mothers' Counsellor if need be. The Nursing Mothers' Association of Australia also publishes two booklets that you might find helpful: *Breastfeeding and Working* and *Expressing and Storing Breastmilk*.

Obviously, it will be much easier to keep feeding your baby only breastmilk if he attends a work-based childcare centre and you can schedule lunchtime or tea-break feeds. However, you can express milk during the day or at night and leave this for the carer to give him.

> 🐦 'My son was in a work-based childcare centre and I was able to go over in work breaks and breastfeed him. I was lucky because it was both very easy and very calm.'

So that you can be reassured that he will drink from a bottle when you aren't available and so that he can get used to it from an early age, start the practice of replacing one of the daytime feeds with a bottle of expressed milk. After a while, increase these feeds to two.

Here are some tips to follow when starting out.

- Your baby might take a bottle of breastmilk from someone else more easily than from you because he is going to associate your smell with your breasts.

- You may need to try differently shaped teats with different-sized holes.

- Some babies simply don't like bottles and will prefer a teaspoon or a cup.

Expressing milk

When you are expressing breastmilk at home you can do so when the baby has finished drinking, early in the morning or late at night, or whenever you have a plentiful supply. However, a big hurdle in expressing breastmilk at work is finding a place to do it. Few women have the luxury of a private office, especially in these days of open plans and goldfish bowls. You're lucky if you can find somewhere to have a sandwich by yourself let alone bare your breasts.

In most places the only available place is the women's toilet, which is neither particularly hygienic nor pleasant. Ask your union rep or your personnel manager if there's a room you could use for half an hour each day. Or perhaps there's a first aid room — and a staff healthy enough not to need to use it.

Try not to feel embarrassed or apologetic about wanting to breastfeed and work or about enquiring about the facilities you need. If other people are embarrassed by your request, it's their problem not yours and until more women start to ask for these simple requirements that enable them to be contented working mothers, things won't start to change.

> 🐦 'I was working as the receptionist for an auto-electrician and I was the only woman. I was considered lucky to have a lady's toilet to myself but it certainly wasn't anything to write home about and definitely no place to express milk. I didn't know how I was going to get around this one but my boss solved the problem for me. He was married to a Nursing Mothers' Counsellor and he let me use his office every day at lunchtime so I could express milk. Life's full of surprises.'

If there isn't somewhere you can comfortably express milk at your workplace, you could try looking for somewhere nearby. Perhaps there's a health centre that could spare a room for a short time each day.

There are some practical matters to think about when you will be expressing breastmilk at work.

- Plan your wardrobe. You don't want to have to sit in your bra and knickers, so dresses aren't a good idea unless they have front openings. Wearing a loose-fitting T-shirt and a skirt tends to be less revealing and a shawl around your shoulders will make you feel more covered up.

- If you feel embarrassed about it, you can disguise your breastmilk in the fridge at work by storing it in a container rather than a bottle or put the bottle in a brown paper bag.

- You will need to carry your milk home in a cold storage pack.

Worry won't help

If it doesn't all go according to plan and what you have to do proves to be too complicated, the best advice is 'Don't worry'. Although easier said than done, remember that your anxiety isn't going to help either you or your baby at this point.

You may find it so difficult to express milk at work that the supply during the day will dwindle. This doesn't mean that your baby's other feeds from the breast will be affected but now may be the time to switch the daytime feeds to formula. Remind yourself that it's not your shortcomings that have made you change tack but it's your situation. The simple fact is that most workplaces don't provide either the facilities or support that breastfeeding mothers need.

Partial breastfeeding

Many women opt for partial breastfeeding once they return to work because it eliminates the pressure of having to express milk regularly.

Well before your return to work, try your baby with a bottle of formula during the time you will later be at work. Express milk after this feed and continue breastfeeding at all other feeds. After a week, increase the formula feeds to two. From about four months, and certainly from six, you can give him solids and drinks from a cup during the day.

Because the quantity of milk is a question of supply and demand, you'll find that it will generally adapt to suit your situation. There will be plenty for the morning and evening feeds and your breasts won't be uncomfortably full during the day.

Storing your breastmilk

You'll need to express about 120 to 150 ml for each feed and, of course, this will increase as your baby grows. By three months he will need 150 to 210 ml in each bottle. Here are some tips about expressing and storing your milk.

• Always sterilise pumps and bottles.

• If most of the baby's feeds are to be given from a bottle, avoid storing in glass as there is some loss of antibodies from breastmilk when stored in glass.

• Mark the containers with the date and time you expressed the milk so you know when to use it by.

• Breastmilk will keep at room temperature in a sealed container for six to ten hours.

• It will keep in the fridge (at the back on the top shelf — not in the door) for five days.

• If the breastmilk hasn't been frozen, stand the container in warm water until it reaches the right temperature for feeding.

• If you are freezing it, wait until it is cold before doing so.

• It will keep in the freezer compartment of the fridge for up to two weeks; in a separate door refrigerator/freezer for three to four months; and in a deep freeze for six months.

• You can add fresh breastmilk to frozen to build up your stores as long as you cool it first and don't leave more than a week between the first lot and the last lot.

• If you put frozen milk in the fridge to defrost, you must use it within 12 hours.

• You can thaw frozen milk by putting the bottle under cold running water and gradually increasing the temperature to warm. Don't heat it on the stove.

• Thawed milk will keep at room temperature for one hour, after which time it should be thrown away.

• Never refreeze defrosted milk.

Partial breastfeeding

Many women opt for partial breastfeeding once they return to work because it eliminates the pressure of having to express milk regularly.

Well before your return to work, try your baby with a bottle of formula during the time you will later be at work. Express milk after this feed and continue breastfeeding at all other feeds. After a week, increase the formula feeds to two. From about four months, and certainly from six, you can give him solids and drinks from a cup during the day.

Because the quantity of milk is a question of supply and demand, you'll find that it will generally adapt to suit your situation. There will be plenty for the morning and evening feeds and your breasts won't be uncomfortably full during the day.

'I breastfed for the six months' maternity leave that I had. Then I would feed him in the morning and again at night and he had bottles of formula during the day. I have to say I went through a pretty uncomfortable few weeks until my milk supply started to settle down but then it was smooth sailing.'

Microwaves and milk

Using the microwave might seem like it's saving time and trouble but it's not all that safe when you are dealing with babies' bottles and milk.

- Microwaves shouldn't be used for sterilising as they don't kill all the harmful bacteria. While there are units available that are designed for sterilising in a microwave, to be on the safe side use a steam steriliser, a chemical sterilant or boil the bottles and teats.
- Warming bottles of formula or breastmilk in a microwave isn't recommended. There can be problems with a difference in temperature between the bottle and teat and bottles have been known to explode. Also, some of the nutrients may be changed or destroyed in the process. The safest way to warm a bottle is still by standing it in warm water.

CHAPTER 12

THE SCHOOL YEARS

Anyone who's been down the childcare path will tell you it's a logistical challenge. Don't think it's over yet. You'll feel as though you could run a military campaign by the time you have all the situations — including the school holidays plus pupil-free school days — covered.

Starting school

Unless your child is attending a private school, the one great advantage in her starting school if she's already been in childcare is that you can now pocket all those fees. The bad news is that it doesn't get any easier for you organisationally. In fact, the childcare can become even more tricky. Now you have at least ten weeks of school holidays a year plus pupil-free days to deal with and, added to that, you have school hours which don't coincide with your working hours.

It's more noticeable to you now, too, that there's a whole population of mothers who don't work and who are available to participate in school activities as well as get their children home before dark in winter. You become more conscious that you are a part-time mother, which enables you to tap into a whole new set of guilt and worries.

Children who have been used to childcare generally slip into school life quite easily but, nevertheless, it is a big step for her and for you. You might like to make arrangements at work either to have some flexibility for a late start and early finish for those first few days or to take one or two days off altogether. Regard this as your first experience of the dilemma of whether to take time off work to attend school activities and functions.

> 'I found it much harder when he started school at the age of five than when he started in childcare at the age of five months. It was like he was going out into the real world and who was going to look after him? The first day I worried that he would be thirsty, hungry and that his shoes would be too tight. Then I told myself "If you keep this up you'll be hospitalised by the end of first term". So then I started to relax a little.'

A participating parent

To maintain some sense of involvement in the school and enable you to feel as though you know what's going on, it helps to attend parent meetings if you can. Sometimes the meetings are held in the evenings and sometimes on weekends — which may seem difficult but it's certainly more manageable than during working hours.

Although you'll almost certainly think that you don't have the time, you'll find that you can manage to squeeze in an hour or so a month when you try. Once you're there, too, you'll discover that many of the parents are in the same working boat as you. It's also a good opportunity for you to make contact with other parents — both working and non-working. Who knows? Perhaps you'll find a soul mate in someone you've only seen before as you rush past each other to collect your children from care at the last minute during the working week.

> 'I've always been involved with the P & C and the after-school care committee. It has allowed me to maintain some connection and I've always thought it a priority.'

Some school events like fundraising meetings, concerts, and sports events are inevitably going to be during your working hours. Obviously you can't attend them all but you'll probably want to make it to some of them. Sometimes your partner may be able to go or other relatives, like aunts and grandparents, might go in your stead, but somewhere along the line you are probably going to have to make the decision to ask for time off if you don't have any flexibility with your working hours.

> 'My daughter was ten years old before I had ever seen her run at the school athletics carnival. I started to feel really bad about it, especially because she was always winning prizes and was so obviously proud of her achievements.'

HOW YOU CAN HELP

You'll feel bad about not being able to help out much with parent activities but there are always little things you can do. Check with whoever's coordinating an event to see if you can contribute by:

- selling raffle tickets;
- helping write promotional pamphlets;
- baking cakes or biscuits for the function;
- donating something to be raffled;
- giving something for a jumble sale.

Care before and after school

If you have to travel a long distance to work, it can be difficult to drop your child at a school near home and still get to work on time. At the other end of the day there are a couple of hours between when school finishes and your working day ends.

> 'Our local school had no before-school care so I had to develop this incredible juggling act. I put him into school near my parents and my mother would drop him at school so I could get to work by nine. This worked okay until he was about seven or eight and then he wanted to have friends over on weekends and they were miles away and he didn't know any of the local kids.'

Some schools have before and after care for children aged 5 to 12 years on the school premises; if not, you can sometimes find it at a local community centre, a nearby childcare centre or through the family day-care scheme. It costs around $6 a session which is about two to three hours in the afternoons.

If you previously used a family day-carer (or a childcare centre) who also provides care before and after school, you might consider keeping your child there. This way you can give your child some continuity while she moves into the wider world of starting at school. It means she can start with or return to the familiarity of her carer each day.

Your other choice is to find a school nearer to work but this poses the same problem as work-based childcare centres — what if you want to change jobs? Also, you'll find as your child gets older, there are several advantages in using a local school.

• She can walk to school alone or with neighbours' children.

• She will develop friendships with local children.

• When she's old enough it's easier for her to come home on her own.

Another possibility for you is to pay another mother at the school to take your child home with her. By putting a notice up or advertising in the school newsletter you might find someone who would be pleased to have the extra cash and some company for her own family.

There are other 'babysitting' options such as employing someone to pick up your child from school and look after her till you get home. Older women who don't want to take on full day care of children are sometimes pleased to find part-time work. Your local paper is a good place to advertise, or ask your neighbours if they know of anyone. Teenage school children, too, often want to earn money and are another avenue of after-school care. Obviously you would want someone who is reasonably mature, so you might want to check with teachers and parents to make sure that this is the right teenager for you.

After-school activities

As your child grows she will begin to develop hobbies and independent interests in things that happen outside school. If you're lucky these interests can be catered for by the after-school care program; otherwise you'll find yourself working out how to get her to Brownies, art classes or basketball training. If these are after your work hours it doesn't pose as much of a problem, although it is yet another thing to fit into the family's tight schedule. If, however, it's an earlier start as many of these things are, you'll need to look at how realistic it is for her to attend.

You might be able to find another child at the school who wants to go and they could travel together either walking or on public transport. A non-working mum might be happy to give her a lift, or if there are two or three and the public transport route is too complicated, you might think of having them share the cost of a taxi to get there.

'My son was begging to take up football but there was no way either my husband or I could get him to midweek training which started at 4.30 p.m. Finally, he was so determined, he organised a lift himself with the mother of another boy at the school. She's happy to take him home afterwards and I pick him up from her after work.'

School holidays

Apart from the fact that there seem to be so many of them, especially with four school terms a year, school holidays involve a change in your routine which inevitably throws you a bit. You have to plan for and then adjust to different daily requirements and times.

Holiday-care programs are available at some schools and provide a range of daily activities such as films, picnics, excursions and centre-based amusements like arts and crafts. Programs are also run by local community centres as well as groups that focus on a particular activity, like an art school running special holiday workshops for children. You'll find these programs advertised in local newspapers or you can try your local council for information.

Some children baulk at spending their holidays back at school but you can usually overcome this by finding an alternative vacation-care program nearby. This can make it more of a holiday for them and gives them the opportunity to spend time with different children and make new friends.

When your child is older there are a range of residential holiday camps, especially sporting ones, that will become available to her. Information about these can be obtained through newspapers, government sport and recreation departments or particular sporting bodies.

Some couples like to stagger their annual leave so that their children get more time at home but then this means less leave left for family holidays together. Some are lucky enough to have grandparents or long-suffering friends whom they can call on.

Unstructured time

A positive side of out-of-school care programs, apart from the fact that they are providing you with care you would have difficulty finding elsewhere, is that most offer stimulating activities as well as playmates for your child. More often than not you'll find that she'll look forward to after-school care and holiday programs and will be reluctant to leave at the end of the day.

The downside is that it makes for a very long day and a very long year in an institutional environment. You feel bad about her going into care at 8 a.m. and leaving at 5.30 or 6 p.m. and doing it for about 46 weeks of the year. It weighs particularly heavily when you recall how much you enjoyed just goofing around as a child.

Just as you feel pressured by time and the number of your commitments, your child's life is also exceptionally busy. It's important to make sure that she has the opportunity to relax and unwind just as you need to at the end of the day. She may need to run and play and let off steam, she might prefer to do some kind of organised activity or she might be happy to simply sit quietly. If she can't get this space at after-school care, she may need it when she gets home. Also think about having at least one unstructured day on the weekend that isn't tied up with commitments and 'have tos'.

'Because we are both freelancers we have been able to juggle the out-of-school time between us with a little backup support from friends. It means that he's been able to have his afternoons free, and as long as he knows who's picking him up and what the routine is, he's happy.'

The horrors of homework

As if there isn't enough going on in your life, you'll also find that you start to suffer from the homework headache. But wait a minute, isn't it supposed to be her homework, not yours?

It's rare to find a working mother who isn't weighed down by the burden of homework and this is partly due to the pressure of time. You get home at around 6 p.m., you have to pay attention to the family's needs — you need to cook a meal, get them bathed and into their pyjamas (and schedule some time in there for yourself). All of a sudden it's 8 p.m. and you find yourself saying 'Have you done your homework?'

In all fairness, it's hard for her to sit down at this time of night, especially when still small, and apply herself to homework. If your child attends after-school care, you might be able to arrange for some homework to be done there — possibly after the children have had a half-hour break. You'll undoubtedly find that other parents will support this move as the last thing anyone wants when they're tired from work is to gird their loins for the homework battle. Supervising or coercing someone into working is not a great way to end your day.

The other part of the homework equation is the child. Books are left at school, instructions forgotten and everything else given priority. The modern-day child doesn't seem to live in fear of the consequences as much as her parents, and the battle to get the work done slips from being hers to yours.

You might find that it eases your guilt if you make up for the time you don't have with your child by taking on the responsibility of her homework. Although it is something that you can spend time together doing, and it's fine for you to take an interest and have some involvement, remind yourself that you aren't doing her any favours by doing her work for her. It's her work and if she makes mistakes that's okay. You need to see it as a part of the process of learning.

Children aren't born knowing how to be organised and it's up to you to set some limits and structures for your child to function effectively and productively. Remind yourself that it's your responsibility to set up the conditions so that she can work easily but then it's over to her.

Homework ground rules

It's a good idea to develop a routine and some ground rules about homework for both of you early.

- Make sure she has a desk or table where she can sit quietly for the allotted time with nothing but the work books.

- Make it a rule that she isn't allowed to move on to other activities such as watching television until the work for that night is completed.

- If she asks for help, help her find the answer but don't tell her the answer. Ask her to tell you how the teacher explained it to her and chances are she'll come up with the solution herself. Also, by doing this you can check that you aren't approaching it from an entirely different angle to the one the teacher used.

- Don't be critical of her work but offer tips and suggestions.

- Remember to praise her when she does the homework at the right time and has taken care in doing it.

'I was so disappointed when the teacher gave my son such a low mark for his latest school project. I'd tried so hard and stayed up so late helping him do it and I was really proud of my input. I think their standards are too high these days.'

Getting to and from school

You get so used to ferrying your children to and from childcare, then school, that sometimes you don't realise that there are simpler solutions. Rather than doing the same trek every day you might want to develop some reciprocal arrangement with other parents at the school and share the morning drop.

At some stage it's going to become feasible for your child to get herself to school and home again but when this happens will depend very much on the child herself, how she feels about it and how you feel about it. She may be able to walk to school, either alone or with other children, or you might be able to find an older child who lives nearby and could catch the same bus or train. When the time comes to go it alone, whether walking or on public transport, take her on a few practice runs so she's familiar with the route.

'I remember the first time he caught the train home alone. I was demented because he had asked me if he could do it and I wasn't quite ready for it. It was all I could do not to leave work and make sure he was okay. I can't tell you how relieved I was when I got his phone call to say he had arrived home safely.'

From after-school care to self-care

If your child has spent her life in childcare and care before and after school, you'll find that by the age of about 12 it may well start to pall for her. This is when you have to start thinking seriously about the 'home alone' routine.

When it happens isn't predictable — it will depend upon your circumstances and your child — but it will be a big step for you both. There are a number of things to consider when thinking about her making the transition from care to going home alone after school.

- What is her level of maturity?

- How capable is she in following directions?

- How high is her level of responsibility?

- Will she be on her own or will other children be there too?

- Is she to be allowed to have friends to visit?

- Is there someone nearby she can call on if need be?

- Is she able to call you and let you know when she has arrived home?

- Does she understand how to deal with calls or visits from strangers?

Home alone checklist

There are several things that you can do to make you feel more at ease about your child going home alone after school.

• Check your home for safety — accidents in the home are probably more cause for concern than anything else.

• If you have concerns about her using some of the appliances, such as the gas stove, make this clear and offer alternatives for making snacks such as the microwave or a jaffle iron.

• Make sure that you have instructed her properly when it comes to security — she shouldn't answer the door to strangers or leave the house unlocked, for example.

• Teach her telephone safety. Many parents tell their children to pretend that a parent can't come to the phone at the moment and to offer to take a message so that a stranger doesn't realise that they're at home on their own.

• Run through safety routines with her and teach her how to use the fire extinguisher and fire blanket and to turn off the electricity.

• Make sure she has both your and your partner's telephone numbers so that she can call you if need be.

• Always have a list of emergency telephone numbers close at hand as well as a backup list with relatives or neighbours she could call on if you can't be contacted.

• Make sure she knows that if she does want to leave the house unexpectedly, she should always telephone you to say why, where and with whom.

• Tell her to look after her house key and always keep it somewhere safe, like on a chain around her neck or attached to her belt.

THE AUTHOR

A love of books drew Belinda Henwood to her first job as a reference librarian but, not one to sit still for very long, her passion for easy-to-understand information moved her into community information work. After the birth of her son, part-time jobs as a research assistant for academics kept the wolf from the door and led her (indirectly) to book publishing, compiling the *Australian Almanac*.

Moving from books to magazines Belinda worked as Features Editor on *New Woman* and then Deputy Editor on *Better Homes and Gardens*. For several years she wrote a question and answer column for the *Women's Weekly* called 'You Asked For It!', and she reviews reference books for the *Sydney Morning Herald*.

Belinda now works as a freelancer from home and is lucky enough to be able to combine in her work her love of writing and editing while staying at home with her family — her son, a dog, a cat and (at last count) four fish.

OTHER TITLES IN THE PARENTING SERIES

THE SECRET OF HAPPY CHILDREN
by Steve Biddulph

What is really happening inside kids' minds? What should parents do about it?

In his bestselling parents' guide, Steve Biddulph teaches parent–child communication in a way that gives you the heart to be more yourself — stronger, more positive and loving, and more sure of yourself. Letting go of old, negative approaches means freeing up more time and energy to enjoy your children and your life.

Topics covered include: stopping tantrums before they start; curing shyness in your children; being a single parent — how to make it easier; kids and TV; how to stop whingeing kids; food and behaviour; the skills of fathering; and the 10 minutes that can save your marriage.

'The best guide to bringing up children we've seen' — *Choice Magazine* Book Club selection

'Humorous, easy to read, sensible and practical' — *The Australian*

MORE SECRETS OF HAPPY CHILDREN
by Steve Biddulph

In this inspirational sequel to *The Secret of Happy Children*, Steve Biddulph shows how parents can put love into action and produce young adults with warm hearts and lots of backbone. A family therapist, educator and father, Steve has worked with families since the 1970s, and talks with thousands of parents every year about what really works.

Topics covered include: how to help toddlers and children feel secure and settled; discipline methods that really work, without hitting or yelling; making sure your love gets through; being the best kind of father; parent pay, the coming innovation; parent power; and how to avoid childcare damaging your child's future.

THE SMART PARENTS GUIDE
by Barbara Briddock

Do you ever feel that life is moving too fast? That meal times, bed times and travelling with children have become a test of endurance? In *The Smart Parents Guide* you will find hundreds of hints and ideas to help you establish and maintain harmony and order in your household during the overpacked years of parenting young children.

Topics covered include: bathing and grooming; bedrooms and bed time; clothes; cooking and meal times; development; families; play time; school, special occasions; travelling and outings; work.

BABIES FROM TOP TO BOTTOM
by Dr Howard Chilton

Enjoy parenthood without panic! A no-nonsense guide to your baby's first year, by the Director of Newborn Care at Sydney's Royal Hospital for Women.

The arrival of your first baby is a wonderful — and terrifying — event! Dr Chilton answers all those questions you suddenly have about what is 'normal' baby behaviour, and shows you how to cope with this massive change in your life and enjoy your baby.

Topics covered include: expectations; the birth; physical examinations of the newborn; bonding; breastfeeding; postnatal depression; the circumcision decision; getting to know your baby; incessant crying; and immunisation.

THE CHILDREN'S SPORTS INJURIES HANDBOOK
by Dr David Kennedy & Peter Fitzgerald

Seven out of ten sports injuries to children can be prevented. This practical guide answers all your questions about prevention and treatment. Essential reading for all parents and coaches of sporting kids.

Topics covered include: warm-up, stretching and strengthening exercises; nutrition; track and field; football and soccer; cricket, baseball, softball and hockey; swimming, surfing, water skiing and sailing; bikes, skateboards, inline skates, horse riding, snow skiing and ice skating; tennis, squash and badminton; netball and basketball, gymnastics and weightlifting.

LEARNING TO TALK, TALKING TO LEARN
by Linda Clark & Catherine Ireland

As parents, the greatest skill we teach our children is talking and communicating. Early speech and language development are the foundations for effective communication skills — skills that are of vital importance to your child for the rest of his or her life, opening doors at school and work and in relationships — and you can help.

Drawing on their experience as speech pathologists and parents, the authors provide information, ideas, activities and skills to prevent speech and language problems and boost language and learning abilities. They show how to use everyday situations and playtime to help your child develop effective communication skills.

YOUR CHILD: EXPECT ADVICE ON RAISING HEALTHY CHILDREN

by Drs Douglas Cohen, Kim Oates & John Yu

This informative and reassuring guide provides parents with clear guidelines and a wealth of commonsense advice on how to raise healthy, happy children. This invaluable book gives parents the information with which they can make informed decisions.

Topics covered include: pregnancy; the new baby; feeding; developmental milestones; immunisation; travelling with children; common behaviour problems; play, TV and toys; handicapped children; childhood illnesses; when to call a doctor; going to hospital; child safety; puberty and adolescence; and emergencies.

BREAST, BOTTLE, BOWL: THE BEST FED BABY BOOK

by Anne Hillis & Penelope Stone

Take the anxiety, mystery and hard work out of feeding babies and children with this enjoyable, easy, stress-free approach to a healthy diet.

Topics covered include: successful breastfeeding; weaning and bottle feeding; introducing solids; how much food and how often; ages and stages; teething; young vegetarians; sample menus; how to cope with fads, food refusal and fussy eaters; and includes easy, delicious and nutritious recipes.

BRINGING UP YOUR TALENTED CHILD

by Geoff Lewis

What every parent wants to know: 'Is my child gifted or talented?' This practical, well-informed and friendly guide shows you how to find out.

Topics covered include: how to identify talent or potential talent in a child; what to do about the talented pre-schooler; how to encourage but not push a talented child; what to look for in a school; how to respond to a talented child's needs; how to help the underachiever; and how to recognise the different types of talent.

This book is a useful handbook for parents and teachers concerned about helping each child fulfil his or her potential.

THE PREGNANCY BOOK

by Doctors & Staff of the Royal Hospital for Women, Sydney

The comprehensive guide to pregnancy, childbirth and the newborn baby, written for all those parents-to-be who have been bombarded with well-meaning (but often conflicting) advice from relatives, friends and colleagues.

Topics covered include: preparing for pregnancy; nutrition and exercise for the pregnant woman; tests to monitor foetal development; prenatal care; normal and problem pregnancies; new trends in childbirth practices; the role of partners; the stages of labour; pain relief in labour; caesarean birth; the newborn infant; breastfeeding; and postnatal care.

COMPUTERS AND KIDS: A PARENT'S GUIDE
by Colin Webb & Wynne Rowe

For children today, growing up with computers is as natural as growing up with books, teddy bears, cars and television.

In this informative, friendly, humorous, accessible and always entertaining book, Colin Webb and Wynne Rowe show you how to integrate your home computer into your children's world in such a way that it fosters their natural curiosity and creativity, helps them develop their individual problem-solving abilities, and encourages them to develop productive attitudes towards using computer technologies, all of which will serve them well throughout their lives.

Topics include: how to teach your child the rudiments of the keyboard and mouse; computer safety; suitable software for children aged one to eight; reading, writing and mathematics software; good and bad computer games; and CD-ROM.

Parenting advice at its most useful, enjoyable and stress-free